Semantics in Political Science Research

Pedro L. Rodr´ýguez Sosa

Dedication

For Daniela

Acknowledgments

As with all intellectual endeavors, this one would not have been possible without the support and contributions of a large group of people to whom I am deeply indebted. In particular I would like to thank:

my committee chair and mentor in the truest meaning of the word, Arthur Spirling;

my dissertation committee, Dimitri Landa, Neal Beck and Chris Dawes, who have provided guidance throughout the final stretch of this project, and especially Jennifer Larson, for her unwavering support throughout my graduate studies;

David J. Halpern, who first introduced me to the study of semantic memory and has remained a close collaborator ever since;

other members of the NYU Politics community, especially professors Pablo Querubín and Eric Dickson, both of whom provided invaluable support at one point or another along this journey, along with my graduate colleagues Abraham Aldama, Mateo Vásquez, Jim Bisbee, Steve Rashin, Jason Guo, Kevin Munger, Alex Siegel, Shoaib Jillani, Denis Stukal, Alessandro Vecchiato and Peter Vining whom provided feedback and encouragement along the way;

the organizers and participants of the conferences and seminar series where I presented earlier versions of this work including Todd Gurecki's Computation and Cognition Lab, John

Jost's Social Justice Lab and Jay van Bavel's Social Perception and Evaluation Lab;

and finally, my family, the bedrock of everything I do.

Abstract

This is a three-part project concerning methods for the study of political semantics —how the 'meaning' of political concepts is represented and organized in memory and implications for political attitudes and behavior. The first chapter proposes a framework for the estimation of group differences in memory representations of political concepts and applies it to evaluate partisan representational differences in the U.S. The second chapter proposes a memory-centered approach to the study of ideology along with the requisite methods for its implementation. The third chapter centers on word embeddings, a deep learning method to estimate word representations from large collections of text. Along with a conceptual overview, it provides practitioners with a series of tests to perform model comparison and validation, including a novel Turing-style test.

Contents

2 In Search of Ideology:

A Memory-Centered Approach   16

3 Word Embeddings: A Framework for Model Comparison and Validation 44

List of Figures

List of Tables

Chapter 1

1.1 Introduction

A growing body of research in the semantic memory literature has identified individual differences in semantic memory organization. What was thought to be largely static and "shared" (Ochsner et al., 2013) has been found to vary as function of expertise (Beilock et al., 2008), culture (Ji, Zhang and Nisbett, 2004; Medin et al., 2006), native versus second language (Borodkin et al., 2016), sensorimotor experience (Yee, 2017), development stage (Markman, 1994) and bodily differences (Thompson-Schill, Kan and Oliver, 2006) among others. Individual differences in semantic memory are likely to have implications for downstream cognitive processes. We suggest that *making attitude judgments* is one such downstream process.

According to constructive models of attitudes from social psychology, making attitude judgments involves sampling (consciously or subconsciously) a limited number of relevant associated concepts (or associations) from memory and computing a summary of the valence of the retrieved associations (Lord and Lepper, 1999; Tourangeau, 1992; Zaller and Feldman, 1992). Although memory retrieval is central to these models, it has never been the direct object of study, instead its role has been limited to providing a conceptual framework to empirical studies of experiment context (Judd et al., 1991; Tourangeau and Rasinski, 1988) with some exceptions (Bhatia, 2017; Lenton, Sedikides and Bruder, 2009). We suggest that semantic memory is likely the source of the considerations and therefore we should expect that differences in semantic memory retrieval will predict differences in the resulting summary and expressed attitudes. In particular, if constructive attitude models are correct, the valences associated with the retrieved associations should explain much of the variance in expressed attitudes.

In this paper we identify differences in representations in a novel domain that we argue is well suited to explore the effect of these differences on attitude judgments: *politics*. In doing so we also showcase a new method to systematically explore differences in representations between groups by estimating semantic representations directly from semantic fluency data.

For the purposes of this paper, we define a subject's semantic representation as an object that constrains the likelihood of concepts or considerations being retrieved from memory. While we focus on semantic network representations in this paper, we leave generalizing our results to alternate models, such as a semantic space model (Landauer and Dumais, 1997) or topic model (Griffiths, Steyvers and Tenenbaum, 2007), to future work. In the paper, we often refer to a representation for a particular concept c, by which we mean the particular region of the semantic representation in the neighborhood of c that is typically retrieved in a task.

1.2   Why Politics?

We test two hypotheses about the relationship between semantic memory and (political) attitudes:

1. Individuals of opposite partisanship (here defined by party identification) have different semantic representations for politically charged concepts.

2. An *individual's* semantic representation for a particular political concept will be predictive of *that individual's* expressed attitude judgments on topics related to that concept.

There are good reasons to expect individual differences in semantic representations as function of partisanship. Political scientists have identified consistent differences in the vocabulary used by political elites (Gentzkow, Shapiro and Taddy, 2016) and media organizations (Morris, 2007) as a function of political affiliation. Moreover, voters' media consumption habits have also been found to show a preference for media outlets perceived to be aligned with currently held political views (Mitchell et al., 2014). Together these findings suggest two individuals of opposite partisanship are likely to have very different linguistic experiences. A fundamental prediction of linguistic based theories of concept acquisition is that differences in linguistic experience will produce different representations (Steyvers, Griffiths and Dennis, 2006; Vigliocco et al., 2009).

Differences in linguistic experience need not be the only source of representational differences in political concepts. Recent work highlights the role of emotions or affect as another type of experiential information relevant in forming semantic representations (Ponari, Norbury and Vigliocco, 2017; Vigliocco et al., 2009), particularly for abstract concepts such as those we are likely to find in politics (e.g. 'freedom', 'equality' etc.). To the extent that individuals experience different emotions when partaking in political activities or encountering political content (Westbury et al., 2015), we should again expect differences in representations to emerge and, more to the point, differences that are likely to be highly relevant for attitude judgments.

1.3   Data

To evaluate these hypotheses, we need to estimate the semantic representations of political concepts for various partisan groups. In the semantic memory literature, semantic spaces are often estimated from large text corpora (Landauer and Dumais, 1997; Lund and Burgess, 1996*b*) or a large set of word associations (Austerweil, Abbott and Griffiths, 2012; De Deyne et al., 2016). These methods are undesirable for our setting since we want to estimate the semantic representations of various sub-populations (members of political parties) for a specific set of concepts, something that would be difficult to do with large text corpora since it is unclear how to select a corpus for each sub-population and topic of interest. In addition, we are interested in topics where we have very weak priors on the extent of the semantic space (relative to the more common concrete topics in psychology like 'fruits') so collecting word associations would require extensive and expensive piloting.

Instead, we build on a literature that estimates semantic representations from the semantic fluency task whereby participants are provided a category label as a cue (e.g. animals, food) and are asked to list as many examples of that category as they can think of within a given time limit and without repetition (Bousfield and Sedgewick, 1944). The semantic fluency task is ideal for our purposes for several reasons: First, in contrast to corpora, semantic fluency lists can be targeted to specific sub-populations of interest, better capturing group idiosyncrasies. Second, it allows us to quickly collect lots of data per subject that is relevant for the given category without the need for priors on which words to use to explore that category. Third, in addition to data on associations, it gives us data on the semantic memory search process which we hypothesize is relevant to predicting attitudes. Fourth, it has been shown to produce better models of semantic representations than single word associations (De Deyne, Navarro and Storms, 2013).

We collected semantic fluency data from 1056 MTurk subjects. As cues we selected words that are politically relevant: `welfare`, `government`, `American values`, `Republican` and `Democrat`. For each cue, subjects were required to respond with associated words without repetitions.[1] Subjects also answered a series of demographic and political attitudes questions, including party identification and ideology.[2] We apply some basic pre-processing to the lists including spelling check, lower casing and singularizing basic plurals (e.g. "patriots" becomes "patriot"). Table 1.1 provides summary statistics of the resulting lists segregating by party identification.

---

[1] Although not a typical category fluency task, the task can be framed as one with the category defined as "words you associate with the cue".

[2] Possible answers to party identification included: "Republican", "Democrat", "Independent", "no preference" and "Other party (please specify)". Ideology was measured on a seven-point Likert scale from "Extremely liberal" to "Extremely conservative" with the option of choosing "Haven't thought much about this".

Table 1.1: summary statistics for concepts lists by party identification after pre-processing.

	Welfare		Government		American Values		Democrat		Republican	
	D	R	D	R	D	R	D	R	D	R
# of unique tokens	1291	912	1552	1085	1507	966	1347	1116	1513	992
Prop. overlap	0.277	0.367	0.305	0.370	0.313	0.339	0.281	0.416	0.303	0.352
Mean list length	14.105	12.848	15.194	14.561	14.354	14.251	14.266	13.696	14.677	14.133
	(4.499)	(4.665)	(4.384)	(4.322)	(4.432)	(4.558)	(4.294)	(4.544)	(4.254)	(4.352)

Notes: D = Democrats and R = Republicans. Prop. overlap corresponds to the ratio of unique tokens to total tokens listed. Numbers in parentheses denote standard deviations of mean list length.

1.4   Method

To estimate partisan differences in representations, we propose a new method that can be used to identify differences in group representations in general. We first estimate separate representations for Democrats and Republicans from their respective semantic fluency lists. Next, we compare the likelihoods of a set of heldout lists under each estimated representation. If there are partisan differences and individuals of the same partisanship overlap more in their representations than individuals of opposing partisanship, then the likelihood of Republican (Democrat) heldout lists should be larger under the Republican (Democrat) representation (within-party) than under the Democrat (Republican) representation (across-party).

We here assume that a semantic representation is a network that is parametrized by an initial probability vector π which contains the probabilities of jumping from the cue word (e.g. "welfare") to a given node (e.g. "poor") and a transition matrix $\mathbf{P}$ where each element of the matrix P_{ij} represents the probability of transitioning from word i to word j (e.g. from "poor" to "help") in one step on the network. For a given π and $\mathbf{P}$, we can compute the likelihood of each list in our dataset and use maximum likelihood or Bayesian inference to infer the parameters of our semantic network. In the past, estimating representations in this way was not possible because the requirement that no word be repeated makes the likelihood of a true generative model non-trivial to compute. Previous models were either non-generative (e.g.

Goñi et al. (2011)) and could not give likelihoods or were biased in their estimation process (Millsap and Meredith, 1987). Only recently has a generative model been proposed which could give likelihoods of producing semantic fluency lists under a set of estimated parameters (which determine the semantic representation). Jun et al. (2015) show that by assuming a particular model for the search process, they can estimate the semantic representation of a group that predicts new lists better than previous biased methods. Building on Austerweil, Abbott and Griffiths (2012), Jun et al. propose a model, called INVITE, whereby retrieval consists of a random walk through the semantic network with words being added to the semantic fluency list every time it reaches a new node. However, due to the constraints of the task, a word that has already been said cannot be repeated so if the random walk reaches a node that corresponds to a repeated word, no word is emitted.

By using the same generative model for both groups, Democrats and Republicans, we are assuming that there are no systematic differences in the search algorithm employed to retrieve associations. We argue that the search algorithm is likely to be a more fundamental cognitive process independent of individual differences in party identification. In Halpern and Rodriguez (2018a) we tested this assumption by comparing the performance of several different models estimated separately on the two groups. The ranking of models according to the log-likelihood of held-out lists was the same for both groups, lending support to our assumption.[3]

---

[3]In this model comparison, we found that INVITE yields better results than many simpler models (including a simple bag-of-words). Since it provides a good description of semantic memory retrieval and has been shown to have nice statistical properties (Jun et al., 2015), we focus on INVITE for our analyses here.

1.5 Individual Differences

We divide up our data into 10 folds, stratifying on party identity. Estimation of the networks

is easier and more reliable if it is limited to words that were included in several subjects'

lists. Given the spread of words that subjects used, we restrict our estimation to the top

30 tokens said for each topic. We estimated a maximum likelihood "population semantic

network" for self-identifying Democrats and Republicans (using LBFGS in rStan Carpenter

et al. (2016)) on a training set of 9 of the folds and then evaluated the log-likelihood of the

heldout fold under each of these two semantic networks. Figure 1.1 plots an example of an

estimated Democrat semantic representation for the concept *Republican*.

Across all ten heldout folds, for all concepts and both parties we find that the within-

party log-likelihood is significantly higher than across-party log-likelihood. As a measure of

how well our model is able to differentiate parties, we can treat our model as a Bayesian

classifier and assign the party with the higher log-likelihood to each list. Figure 1.2 plots the

average accuracy of this classifier by concept. In all cases, the classifier is able to perform

significantly better than an 'all same class' classifier.[4] The accuracy score in this case has a

theoretically substantive interpretation: the larger the representational differences between

groups, the easier it is for a classifier to distinguish between a Republican and Democrat

resulting in a larger accuracy score, for political scientists this can be understood as a

measure of "polarization" (Peterson and Spirling, 2018). To further benchmark our results

we applied our method to estimate semantic representations by gender rather than by party.[5]

Figure 1.2 also plots the accuracy scores by gender for each concept. Except for the concept

---

[4]Since our sample is stratified by party, an 'all same class' classifier achieves an accuracy score of 0.5.

[5]Gender has also been previously identified as a potential source of differences in semantic representations (Capitani, Laiacona and Barbarotto, 1999).

"Republican", our results suggest no significant gender differences in representations for our set of cues. Overall we find evidence that Democrats and Republicans do indeed strongly differ in their representations for these concepts.

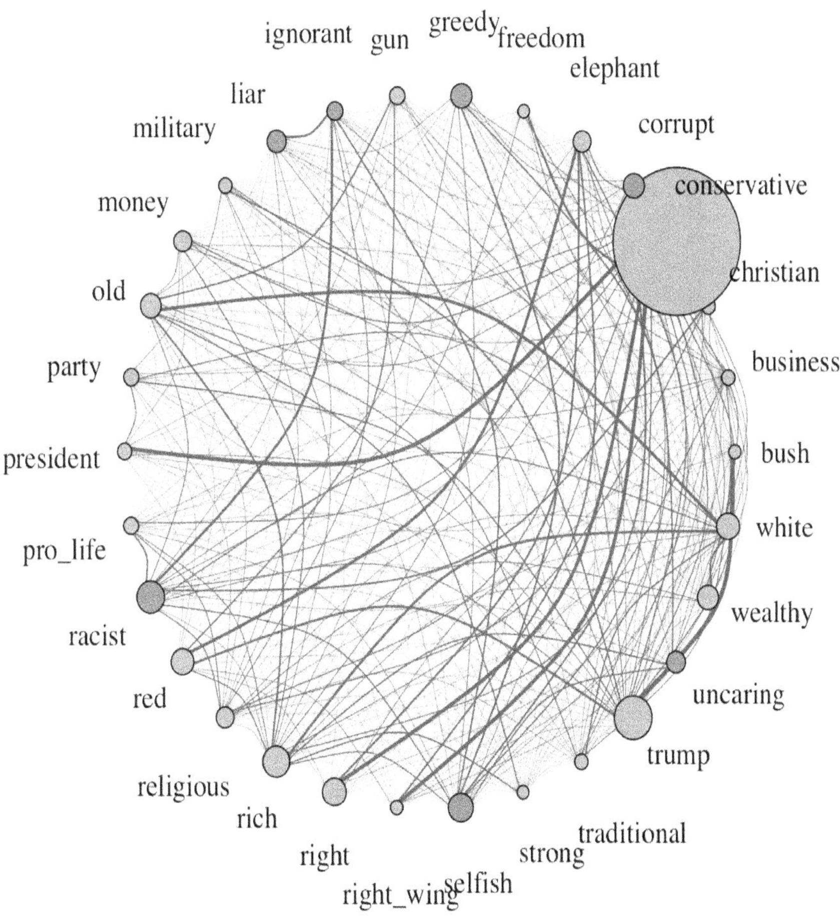

Figure 1.1: Democrat network for the concept "Republican"
Note: Clusters of concepts as estimated by the Walktrap algorithm are indicated by color.

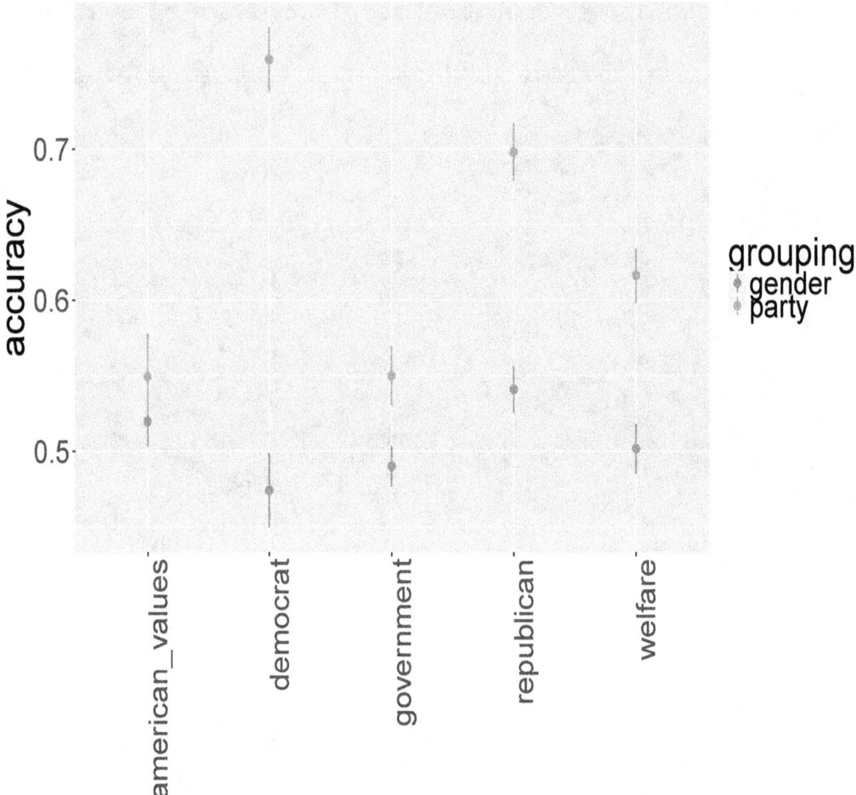

Figure 1.2: Model accuracy in discriminating between Democrat and Republican heldout subjects

1.6 Individual Differences and Attitudes

To explore whether retrieved semantic associations are predictive of attitude judgments we
also collected data on general attitudes toward the government's role in providing services
(related to the concept *government*) and its role in guaranteeing a minimum standard of
living (related to the concept *welfare*). Both attitude questions were on a seven-point Likert
scale and were recoded to range from -3 (extremely liberal position) to 3 (extremely con-

servative position).[6] We hypothesized the difference in the log-likelihoods of an individual's

category fluency data under the Republican (LL_R) and Democrat (LL_D) models, a quantity

we term *concept partisanship*, should be predictive of that individual's attitude judgments

(using the representations for *welfare* for the question on welfare and *government* for the

question on government services). The more negative (positive) the concept partisanship for

subject i for concept c, the better that subject's fluency list approximates the Democrat's

(Republican's) estimated representation. Table 1.2 reports our results of including concept

partisanship as a regressor of expressed attitudes. Concept partisanship is significant even af-

ter controlling for party affiliation and ideology suggesting our representations are capturing

more than group affiliation.

According to constructive models of attitudes, when responding to a survey question

on attitudes individuals sample from memory, compute a statistic (e.g. an average) of the

valences of the sampled information and respond accordingly. Building on this intuition we

next asked how much predictive leverage can we get from simply using the average valence

of the retrieved lists to predict attitude judgments. This requires we first attach a valence

to the retrieved words which we do using a set of $13,915$ valence norms from Warriner,

Kuperman and Brysbaert (2013). These valence norms range from a low of 1 ("unhappy")

to a high of 9 ("happy") and subjects are instructed to respond how a word makes them

feel. We emphasize this is an imperfect measure of valence to the extent that the valence

of a word likely changes as a function of context and party affiliation yet it provides for an

acceptable first approximation. Our results confirm that average valence of the retrieved

lists is a significant predictor of expressed attitudes consistent with constructive models of

---

[6]Both attitude questions were taken from the American National Elections Studies (ANES) Survey.

attitudes (Table 1.2).

Table 1.2: Attitudes towards welfare as a function of concept partisanship and average valence

	Dependent variable: attitudes toward expanding welfare			
	(1)	(2)	(3)	(4)
Concept Partisanship	0.335***	0.097***		
	(0.023)	(0.028)		
Average Valence			−0.662***	−0.307***
			(0.069)	(0.058)
Party (Republican = 1)		0.242		0.522**
		(0.283)		(0.261)
Ideology		0.487***		0.451***
		(0.063)		(0.063)
Constant	−0.123*	−0.094	2.952***	1.233***
	(0.070)	(0.152)	(0.347)	(0.319)
Observations	575	573	591	589
R^2	0.270	0.453	0.136	0.449
Adjusted R^2	0.269	0.450	0.134	0.446

Notes: *p<0.1; **p<0.05; ***p<0.01
Ideology ranges from -3 (extremely liberal) to 3 (extremely conservative).

1.7 Valence Clusters

Previous studies using semantic fluency tasks have observed that subjects produce items in bursts of semantically related words (Troyer, Moscovitch and Winocur, 1997), consistent with semantic memory being organized in clusters of semantically related concepts. Given we found average valence of retrieved lists to be predictive of attitudes, we wondered whether valence serves as an organizing principle of semantic memory alongside semantic similarity (Osgood, Suci and Tannenbaum, 1978; Westbury et al., 2015). One way of testing this hypothesis is to first assess whether clusters are present in our estimated representations and, given clusters are present, whether nodes within clusters tend to align according to valence. To evaluate the presence of clusters in our estimated representations we applied the

Walktrap algorithm (Steinhaeuser and Chawla, 2010). Intuitively this algorithm identifies as clusters the densely connected regions of a graph in which simulated random walks tend to get "trapped".[7] Figure 1.1 plots the estimated Democrat semantic representation for the concept *Republican* with different colors representing different clusters. The *Walktrap* algorithm identifies three distinct clusters. We draw the reader's attention to the highly negatively valenced *green* cluster vis-a-vis the other relatively more neutral clusters. Using the same valence norms we used in the regressions above, we can estimate mean valence by cluster (see Table 1.3). The green cluster (consisting of the words "corrupt", "greedy", "ignorant", "liar", "racist", "selfish" and "uncaring") is significantly more negatively valenced than the other two clusters. We see this as suggestive evidence of valence serving as an important organizing dimension of semantic memory, a result meriting further research.

Table 1.3: Mean valence by cluster in Figure 1.1

	yellow	blue	green
mean	5.62	5.77	2.68
valence	(1.0250)	(1.390)	(0.567)

1.8 Discussion

We have outlined a method to explore differences in semantic representations between groups and applied it to a novel domain: politics. We hypothesized that individuals of opposite partisanship have different semantic representations for politically relevant concepts. In our data, we find evidence of differences across several political concepts although the magnitude of the difference is found to vary by concept, with concepts related to self-identity (Democrat and Republican) showing the largest differences. We also hypothesized that an individual's

---

[7]The algorithm works best with small step sizes. We limit our random walk to 3 steps.

semantic representation of a politically relevant concept is predictive of that individual's attitudes toward topics related with that concept. Again, we find strong confirmatory evidence for this hypothesis. Finally we also found evidence consistent with valence playing an important role, alongside semantic similarity, in the organization of semantic memory.

We began by arguing that partisan differences in representations are likely to have emerged as a result of differences in the linguistic and emotional experiences of Democrats and Republicans. We now proceed to sketch out a more general theory of the relationship between semantic memory and attitudes. We hypothesize, that there might be a computational reason for these differences that further constrains how representations develop and change. The organization of semantic memory is thought to be optimized for making efficient and accurate knowledge-based inferences and predictions (e.g. top-down perception (Biederman, Kubovy and Pomerantz, 1981) and linguistic prediction (Steyvers, Griffiths and Dennis, 2006). This is consistent with the fact that semantic memory has been found to be organized according to similarity in sensorimotor experiential data and language-based distributional data (Andrews, Vigliocco and Vinson, 2009). However, many studies have suggested valence as another important dimension of semantic organization (Osgood, Suci and Tannenbaum, 1978; Westbury et al., 2015), potentially resulting from co-occurrence statistics of affective experience (Vigliocco et al., 2009).The fact that many of our most discriminating tokens are valenced and that similarly valenced nodes seem to cluster together is consistent this theory. This begs the questions: what use is valence as an organizing principle? We hypothesize that semantic memory is also optimized for efficient and consistent evaluative judgments under limited resources. If evaluative judgments do indeed follow a sampling like process then it makes sense for valence to play an organizing role lest individuals produce an endless stream of conflicting evaluations. We see this as a line research meriting greater attention and believe politics as a domain is ideally suited to this task. More generally we hope the method outlined above provides a basic framework to begin to quantitatively explore the relationship between semantic memory and attitudes and that our promising results serve to highlight the potential returns to cognitive science of branching into less traditional domains.

Chapter 2

In Search of Ideology:

A Memory-Centered Approach

2.1   Introduction

Are voters ideological? According to Converse's seminal piece (Converse, 1962) and the many studies that followed in its footsteps the answer is a resounding no, to the point that some researchers classified the study of ideology as futile (Kinder, 1982).[1] This conclusion however, is contingent on a specific definition of ideology, namely as a system of beliefs that are referentially defined with respect to phenomena external to the individual, usually a set of culturally accepted ideas reflecting a combination of elite discourse and 'expert knowledge'. This line of thinking is reflected in propositions such as: if voter i believes X, then she must also believe Y. The fact that she doesn't believe both X and Y is taken as evidence of ideological inconsistency. An alternative conclusion that may be drawn from these findings is that ideology thus defined does not provide an adequate conceptual framework with which to study the constraints, if any, that characterize how voters think about politics much less their political behavior (Rosenberg, 1987). We posit the study of ideology stands to

---

[1]For a recent iteration of this argument see Kinder and Kalmoe (2017).

benefit from doing away with the confines of a normatively prescribed belief structure, while maintaining the underlying notion of ideology as a source of constraints or structure in how people think about politics. But where should we look for this structure?

All theories of attitude judgments posit some role for memory retrieval, be it of 'evaluative tags' directly associated with the attitude object (Fazio, 2001, 2007), knowledge or considerations relevant to making an evaluation (Conrey and Smith, 2007; Gawronski and Bodenhausen, 2007; Tourangeau, 1992; Zaller and Feldman, 1992) or, more likely, a combination of the two (Cunningham et al., 2007; Eagly and Chaiken, 2007; Hastie and Pennington, 1989; Lodge, Taber and Weber, 2006). Retrieval is necessarily a function of *memory organization*, semantic memory to be terminologically precise —the part of memory that allows us to interact with the world in a knowledge-based manner.[2] Insofar as we understand ideology as constraints in how people think and come to evaluative judgments about politics, it is in the organization of semantic memory that our search may be most fruitful.

With some notable exceptions (see for example Szalay, Kelly and Moon (1972)), memory organization has received relatively little attention in the study of ideology.[3] Moreover, while references to memory organization are more common in the study of attitude judgments, it has failed to translate into corresponding methodological innovations. This may in part be due to the persistent belief that the human mind lies beyond our reach, justifying a focus on observable behavior (Mannheim, 1936; Skinner, 1963; Watson, 2017). More often than not, memory is treated as a black box or only partially measured — e.g. implicit association test.[4]

Our objective in this paper is to propose an alternative approach to the study of ideology, one centered in memory organization. Starting with the premise that voters' attitudes are a reflection of how their semantic memory is organized, we propose defining ideology as *shared*

---

[2]We use the words constraints and structure interchangeably. Moreover, whenever we write memory we are referring to semantic memory.

[3]Sociologists and social psychologists have been more receptive to the study of memory organization although often under different guises: *cognitive organization* (Newcomb, Turner and Philip, 1965), *conceptual organization* (Harvey, Hunt and Schroder, 1961), *cognitive systems* (Krech, Crutchfield and Ballachey, 1962) and *schemas* (DiMaggio, 1997) among others.

[4]The implicit association test measures strength of associations in memory (Greenwald et al., 2009), but it requires a priori assumptions on which items to test and only provides information on that very limited set of items.

constraints on the organization of political concepts in semantic memory. Using semantic fluency data, we first evaluate the above premise and then provide evidence for the presence of constraints in semantic memory organization. Our results show semantic memory organization is indeed predictive of attitudes. Moreover, we find evidence of constraints in the organization of political concepts. According to these results, the response to our motivating question is a tentative yes. We conclude by examining the correspondence between ideological self-identification measures and memory organization. Overall, the proposed approach shows significant promise in the study of ideology and attitudes more broadly.

2.2   From Ideology as Information to Schemas

Information plays a prominent role in Converse's understanding of belief systems —his preferred term for ideology (Converse, 1962). It is information about *"what goes with what and why"* that constrains voters' political beliefs. Empirically this translates into comparing voters' expressed beliefs, as registered through both closed- and open-ended survey responses, with expected responses based on a normative organization of beliefs. For example, we may expect a voter that is in favor of increasing unemployment benefits to also support increasing spending in government provided services —both positions presumably consistent with a Liberal ideology. Employing this approach, Converse goes on to find that most voters —in his representative sample— exhibit 'ideological inconsistencies' and a general lack of political knowledge. Only a minority of voters, the politically informed, can be said to be *ideological.* Converse would go on to characterize the majority of voters as having non-attitudes (Converse, 1970). Subsequent studies adopting a similar approach echoed Converse's pessimistic view of voter competence (Freeder, Lenz and Turney, 2019; Kinder and Kalmoe, 2017; Lupia, McCubbins and Arthur, 1998).[5]

---

[5]This less than optimistic view of the 'average citizen' was far from new. In reference to the 'democratic man' Plato says: "He often engages in politics, leaping up from his seat and saying and doing whatever comes into his mind. If he happens to admire soldiers, he's carried in that direction, if money-makers, in that one. There's neither order nor necessity in his life, but he calls it pleasant, free, and blessedly happy, and he follows it for as long as he lives." (Ferrari and Griffith, 2000).

Borrowing from the decision-making literature in psychology (Kahneman et al., 1982), an influential group of studies portray voters as cognitive misers who substitute encyclopedic knowledge for heuristics when engaging in political decision-making (Fiske and Taylor, 1991; Lau and Sears, 1986). These include work on brands (Goggin, Henderson and Theodoridis, 2016), partisan stereotypes (Rahn, 1993) and issue and trait ownership (Egan, 2013; Hayes, 2005; Petrocik, 1996). These studies are generally less pessimistic in their conclusions yet their approach can still be characterized as referential. In effect, they 'lower the bar' for ascertaining voter competence, but a bar is still present. This 'referential' approach to the study of ideology is partly predicated on the belief that for voters to hold elites accountable, there must be some correspondence between the interplay of ideas as presented by political elites and voters' understanding. This is warranted if we were solely interested in the diffusion of information from elites to citizens or indeed in evaluating voter competence. However, if our goal is to evaluate the presence or lack thereof of constraints in how voters think about politics, it seems misguided to ex-ante confine ourselves to a set of normatively defined constraints.

With this intuition in mind, a number of researchers, inspired by the 'cognitive revolution' of the 1950s and 60s, turned to the mind in search of constraints, exploring the role of 'cognitive structures of organized prior knowledge' most commonly referred to as *schemas* or *schemata* (Fiske and Linville, 1980). Empirically this meant searching for latent structures in observed attitude evaluations as opposed to comparing subject responses to a set of normatively defined responses.[6] This work identified several *schemas* that evidenced an underlying structure to attitudinal survey responses (Conover and Feldman, 1984; Lau, 1989; Miller, Wattenberg and Malanchuk, 1986). However, a lack of consensus as to how to approach the measurement of schemas along with skepticism as to the value added of adopting the cognitive framework meant this line of research never truly achieved its lofty expectations, with some political psychologists dismissing it as "old wine in new bottles" (Kuklinski,

---

[6]A similar 'agnostic' approach can be found in social psychology (Baldassarri and Goldberg, 2014; Boutyline and Vaisey, 2017).

Luskin and Bolland, 1991). The obvious empirical challenges notwithstanding, the intuition that to understand political behavior we need to understand how voters "picture the world around them" (Lodge et al., 1991) is well founded.[7] In our own attempt to formalize this intuition, we will draw from the literature on how people come to make attitude judgments, the very process ideology is supposed to constrain.

2.3 Attitudes: Stored, Constructed or Both?

Attitudes had long been conceptualized as latent constructs that capture peoples' enduring dispositions toward attitude objects —persons, groups, ideas etc. (Allport, 1979; Cook and Flay, 1978; Petty and Cacioppo, 2012). Assuming away measurement error, this perspective implies responses to attitudinal measures, be they implicit or explicit, should reflect the stability of the underlying construct. Much empirical evidence suggests otherwise, from the inter-temporal instability noted by Converse and others (Converse, 1962; Zaller et al., 1992), to the influence of seemingly irrelevant contextual factors on survey responses including among others, question wording (Bradburn, 1982; Reid, 1983), question order (Schuman, 1992) and survey location (Berger, Meredith and Wheeler, 2008). This incriminating evidence resulted in a proliferation of new attitude models.[8]

At one end of the continuum attitudes continue to be thought of as enduring evaluative dispositions *stored* in long-term memory. These models differ from the traditional view in that they allow for some instability in responses through differential accessibility to stored attitudes (Fazio, 1989); allowing an attitude object to be linked to more than one evaluative tag (Petty, Briñol and DeMarree, 2007) or simply acknowledging that there may

---

[7]The distinction between a referential approach to the study of ideology and an 'ideology in the mind' approach echoes that between cognitive semantics (Gärdenfors, 2004; Jackendoff, 1983; Lakoff, 2008; Langacker, 2002) and realists theories of semantics (Putnam, 1975) regarding the relation between meaning and the outside world. For 'cognitivists' *meaning lies in the mind,* that is, it is subjective and can exist independently from any objective truth imposed by the 'outside' world. For 'realists' meaning and reality are inseparable. A consequence of the latter viewpoint is that a majority of individuals do not know the 'true meaning' of most words, this is a privilege reserved to the experts of different fields. Thus a chemist knows the 'true' meaning of **gold** as a chemical element and the Political Scientist the 'true' meaning of **Democracy** as a system of governance.

[8]Measurement error resulting in part from an imperfect mapping between underlying attitudes and the format and language of surveys was proposed as one potential source of instability (Achen, 1975; Dean and Moran, 1977; Feldman, 1989). However, measurement error could at best account for half of the observed variance.

be several paths for respondents to arrive at an answer (i.e. stable-attitude models apply to strongly held attitudes).[9] At the other end of the continuum expressed attitudes are portrayed as *constructed* from currently accessible information (Conrey and Smith, 2007; Gawronski and Bodenhausen, 2007; Schwarz, 2007; Tourangeau, Rips and Rasinski, 2000; Wilson and Hodges, 1992; Zaller and Feldman, 1992). According to these models —jointly known as constructionist models— responses will ultimately reflect a summary of whatever is sampled. The lack of stability and structure observed in attitudinal surveys is the result of this sampling being stochastic. More recently, consensus has been shifting towards hybrid models that allow for both stored evaluations and other relevant cognitions to play a role (Cunningham et al., 2007; Eagly and Chaiken, 2007; Hastie and Pennington, 1989; Lodge, Taber and Weber, 2006). One way in which stored evaluations can play a role in constructionist models is by delimiting the sampling process, with less consolidated attitudes requiring greater effort in sampling nearby considerations.

This shift in how we conceive of attitudes has important implications for measurement (Gawronski, 2007). In a stored attitudes world, attitudes represent a fixed target at which we can aim our measurement tools. The goal of measurement in this case is precision. In a constructed attitudes world, we are no longer aiming at one target but rather at a moving object which may nevertheless have some probability distribution associated with it. In this case any single measure, be it implicit or explicit, while perhaps informative of one part, may lead to a mischaracterization of the whole. Instead, measurement should be aimed at 'mapping' the space from which items are retrieved. This 'space' is memory, semantic memory to be more terminologically precise.

---

[9]These other paths include relating an attitude object to a global evaluation linked to the object or to the category an object belongs to (Fazio, 2007; Sanbonmatsu and Fazio, 1990); resorting to an on-going tally that is continuously updated as new information on the attitude object is encountered (Lodge, McGraw and Stroh, 1989); appealing to general values and pre-dispositions (Haidt, Joseph et al., 2007).

2.4 Semantic Memory

Semantic memory refers to the part of memory where concepts and word meanings are stored.[10] The latter are the inputs we use on a daily basis to interact with the world in a knowledge-based manner, they underpin our ability to recognize objects, make inferences and, not least, interpret language (Yee, Jones and McRae, 2018). Concepts and word meanings are stored in the form of *mental representations*.[11] In this paper our 'window into the mind' is language. We therefore use representations and *semantic representations* interchangeably.[12]

2.4.1 Modeling

As is common in the literature, we model semantic memory as an N-dimensional real-valued vector-space S_i. The subscript is there to highlight that this space is specific to the individual. Words are represented as points —$1 \times N$ vectors— on this space. The dimensions of S_i together make up the different dimensions along which *meaning* can vary.[13] Distance in this space is proportional to semantic similarity.

2.4.2 Measurement

One approach to the measurement of representations, and memory organization more broadly, is brain imaging (e.g. fMRI, MEG), wherein representations are measured as brain pattern activation —changes in blood-oxygen levels or magnetic fields— as subjects are shown words, videos or audios. Advancements in imaging technology has increased its appeal in the study memory representations (see e.g. Dikker and Pylkkänen (2013); Huth et al. (2016)) yet,

---

[10]Psychologists distinguish between declarative —consciously accessible— and non-declarative memory. Within declarative memory, they distinguish between semantic and episodic memory. Episodic memory refers to memories of autobiographical events (Reisberg, 2013). These should be understood as theoretical constructs, not as separable regions of the human brain.

[11]At a neurophysiological level, representations are a series of chemically and electrically induced neuron firings.

[12]The representation of non-linguistic entities such as objects, actions etc. are referred to as *conceptual representations* (Murphy, 2004). The relationship between semantic and conceptual representations is an open question in the study of semantic memory (Vigliocco and Vinson, 2007), yet it is not uncommon for them to be treated interchangeably.

[13]The representation for the word `apple` for example, is likely to have non-zero values on dimensions related to *space* —an apple is round— *function* —an apple is nutritious— and *taste* or *valence* —an apple is tasty, we like apples.

despite the allure of what is presumably high internal validity, the technology remains too expensive and intrusive to be scalable. Moreover, imaging requires a strong theory as to 'where' in the brain to look. As an alternative, psychologists have long relied on drawing inferences from behavioral tasks or linguistic output. Behavioral tasks, including lexical decision tasks (Meyer and Schvaneveldt, 1971; Schvaneveldt and Meyer, 1973), implicit association test (Greenwald, McGhee and Schwartz, 1998) and categorization tasks (Shepard, Hovland and Jenkins, 1961), generally require a priori assumptions on which items to test limiting inferences to this reduced set of items.

The last two decades have seen significant progress in the development of computational methods that "learn" the *semantic representation* of words from natural language datasets. Among these, *distributional semantic models* including Latent Semantic Analysis (LSA) (Landauer and Dumais, 1997), topic models (Blei, Ng and Jordan, 2003) and, more recently, word embeddings (Mikolov, Chen, Corrado and Dean, 2013; Pennington, Socher and Manning, 2014) have shown remarkable success in capturing 'human' semantics.[14] The main advantage of these methods is their scalability to huge vocabularies and corpora. However, this scalability comes at the cost of flexibility —in a way, they are good for studying aggregates less so for studying targeted differences. These methods are ill suited to target specific concepts, for particular sub-populations and, more problematically, account for context-dependence.

A more flexible alternative is the semantic fluency task, wherein subjects are provided a cue (e.g. `New York`, `Democrat` etc.) and are asked to list as many associations as they can think of within a given time limit and without repetition (Bousfield and Sedgewick, 1944). The retrieval process that generates the set of associations has long been thought of as a process of *spreading activation* through interconnected nodes with semantic similarity determining the probability of conscious retrieval (Collins and Loftus, 1975; Quillan, 1966).[15]

---

[14]DSMs all draw from the same basic principle, namely that words with similar distributions in natural language —measured by co-occurrences with other words within a researcher defined context— will tend have similar semantic representations, an idea formalized in the 'distributional hypothesis' (Firth, 1957a; Harris, 1954; Wittgenstein, 2010).

[15]The order in which items are retrieved is considered to be indicative of proximity in semantic memory. There are obvious

Which words come to mind when thinking about a given cue will depend on context. Any two words can be compared along any number of dimensions. Take the words `Trump` and `Obama` for example, they are clearly similar along some dimensions —e.g. both are associated with `presidency`— but may be very different along others —e.g. a valence dimension. The role of context can be thought of as determining dimension saliency (Gärdenfors, 2004; Nosofsky, 1986). It is possible to make inferences on which dimensions were most salient for retrieval in a given context by comparing the set of retrieved associations. Below we detail a more rigorous approach.[16] The semantic fluency task offers a good middle ground between the limited scope of imaging and behavioral measures and the 'over-aggregation' of corpus-based distributional semantic models, as it is both efficient —can quickly collect lots of data on memory representations— targetable —can be targeted at specific sub-populations— and easily customizable —can include experimental treatments (e.g. be preceded by a priming treatment).

2.5   Theory: Ideology as Constraints on Memory Organization

Our starting premise is clear: voters' attitudes are a reflection of how their semantic memory is organized. In particular, expressed attitudes —i.e. responses to survey questions— will be bound by this structure. With this premise in mind, we define ideology as *shared constraints on the organization of political concepts in semantic memory.*[17] In common with the referential perspective described above, ideology is understood as *constraining* thought. Moreover, it is understood to be social, insofar as it is believed to emerge primarily through social interactions.[18] However, it differs in that constraints are not defined in reference to some normative understanding of *what goes with what and why.* Our empirical strategy is

---

parallels with the distributional hypothesis (Harris, 1954).

  [16]The semantic fluency task is particularly suitable to study how context —e.g. following a prime— affects retrieval. This is much harder to do with corpus-based methods.

  [17]This definition echoes that by Denzau and North (1994) who refer to ideologies as "the shared framework of mental models that groups of individuals possess that provide both an interpretation of the environment and a prescription as to how that environment should be structured".

  [18]There may be idiosyncratic structure that is relevant for political decision-making but which is not shared. Under the proposed definition this is not ideology.

as follows. First, we empirically evaluate our starting premise, that is, whether memory organization is indeed predictive of attitude judgments. We are really only interested in the study of ideology to the extent that it allows us to better understand political behavior. As such, if our starting premise does not hold, the proposed approach loses much of its appeal. Having shown this correspondence we go on to evaluate the presence of shared constraints. Before discussing the specifics of our methods, we lay out the theoretical justification along with the corresponding testable hypotheses for each of these steps.

2.5.1   Memory Organization and Attitude Judgments

Semantic memory is thought to be optimized for making efficient and accurate knowledge-based inferences and predictions including top-down perception —e.g. recognizing a face— (Biederman, Kubovy and Pomerantz, 1981) and linguistic prediction —processing of meaning (Steyvers, Griffiths and Dennis, 2006). Different memory-based experiments show significant correlations between retrieval and both sensorimotor experiential data and language-based distributional data, indicating both play a role in the organization of semantic memory (Andrews, Vigliocco and Vinson, 2009). Several studies have also pointed to valence —in the affective sense— as an organizing principle, specially for abstract concepts (e.g. liberty, equality, fairness etc.) (Osgood, Suci and Tannenbaum, 1978; Vigliocco et al., 2009; Westbury et al., 2015). As it pertains to the semantic representation of words, similarly valenced words —words that are both associated with either positive or negative emotions— tend to be more proximate in semantic memory than oppositely valenced words. Halpern and Rodriguez (2018c) propose that valence as an organizing principle is consistent with semantic memory also being optimized to make efficient and relatively stable evaluative judgments under limited resources. This suggests that valence will be a particularly salient dimension —recall retrieval varies as a function of dimension saliency— for attitude objects, for example, political cues. Moreover, the representation of attitude objects in memory will be predictive of attitudes toward those objects. Importantly, if the organization of political concepts in semantic memory is constrained, that is, if voters are ideological according to the proposed definition, then we'd expect the semantic representation of any political cue to be predictive of attitudes broadly, not just attitudes specific to that cue. This is the memory equivalent of: if voter i believes X, then she likely also believes Y. We summarize these arguments in the following testable hypotheses:

Hypothesis 1: the valence dimension is highly salient in the retrieval of associations of political concepts.

Hypothesis 2: voters' representations of political concepts are predictive of political attitudes broadly.

2.5.2 Shared Representations

Semantic memory organization is grounded in experience. This includes sensory-motor (Wolk, Coslett and Glosser, 2005), linguistic (Steyvers, 2010) and, according to more recent research, emotional experience (Kousta et al., 2011; Vigliocco et al., 2009). Individuals with common experiences will tend to have overlapping representations. There are good reasons to expect clusters of individuals with similar semantic representations of political concepts. From a top-down —elite-driven— perspective, several authors have pointed to elite discourse as an important source of information for political semantics (Hart, 2010; Lau, 1986; Van Dijk, 2008; Zaller et al., 1992). Differences in the language used by elites of opposing political views when discussing the same topics may drive differences in voters' own semantic representations (Gentzkow, Shapiro and Taddy, 2016; Jensen et al., 2012; Peterson and Spirling, 2018).

From a bottom-up —voter-driven— perspective, Walsh and Cramer (2004) stress the role of social interactions in shaping 'meaning', while Sperber (1996) introduces the concept of *cultural representations*, in reference to representations that "get communicated repeatedly, and end up being distributed throughout the group, and thus have a mental version in most of its members". Combined with evidence that people tend to interact more with peers that share political preferences (Barberá, 2015; McPherson, Smith-Lovin and Cook, 2001), we should expect differences to be self-reinforcing and spread across different concepts thereby creating ideology-like constraints. The advent of social media may intensify this process (Settle, 2018). To be clear: *one shared semantic representation an ideology doth not make.* If the organization of political concepts in semantic memory is 'ideologically' constrained, then we expect two voters that have a similar representation for one political cue to be more likely to overlap in their representations of other political cues. Be it through elite- or voter-driven diffusion, the corresponding testable hypothesis is that:

Hypothesis 3: the organization of semantic memory is not entirely idiosyncratic. Instead we should observe clusters of voters that overlap in their representations of a broad range of political concepts.

2.6   Data

Our data consists of a series of semantic fluency tasks performed by workers on Amazon Mechanical Turk.[19] As cues we selected five political words: `government`, `American values`, `Democrat`, `Republican` and `welfare`. The tasks were programmed in Qualtrics and participants were provided a link to the survey. The survey began with the five tasks, with the order of the cues randomized, followed by a series of demographic questions and questions on political preferences, including party affiliation, ideology and two attitudinal questions on government services and welfare (see Supporting Information for task wording and attitude questions).[20][21] We apply some minor pre-processing to the lists including spelling check, lower-casing, singularizing basic plurals (e.g. "patriots" becomes "patriot") and checking for collocations (e.g. some subjects may have written `red-tape` while others wrote `redtape`). We further subset the feature set to words mentioned by at least 5 subjects. In total 1056 respondents participated in the survey. As is common with MTurk samples, self-identified

---

[19]Data was collected during the months of February and March 2017.

[20]All questions were taken from the ANES.

[21]The protocol for this data collection received IRB approval (application IRB-FY2016-1310).

Liberals, 37% of the sample, far outnumber self-identified Conservatives, 21% of the sample, with moderates making up the remaining 42%.[22] Table 2.1 provides basic summary statistics for each cue (values in parentheses are standard deviations).[23]

	Total Words	Unique Words	Words w. Min Count	Avg. List Length	Mean Lists per Word
government	13803	2875	437	13.10	4.80
				(4.89)	(16.0)
American values	13045	2731	420	12.40	4.78
				(4.71)	(17.4)
Democrat	12585	2992	476	12.00	4.21
				(4.72)	(15.7)
Republican	13133	3020	468	12.50	4.35
				(4.78)	(16.7)
welfare	12166	2470	388	11.60	4.93
				(4.83)	(19.7)

Table 2.1: Summary Statistics by Cue

2.7 Methods

For each cue we generate a document feature matrix —each subject is a row and the features are the listed words. We reduce the dimensionality of this matrix using principal component analysis (PCA) keeping the first N principal components that jointly capture 80% of the variance —all results are robust to the choice of dimensions.[24] The output of this procedure is, for each cue, a set of N-dimensional vectors, one for each subject. We will refer to these vectors as *revealed representations*. We now detail the methods used to evaluate each of our hypotheses.

2.7.1 Memory Organization and Attitude Judgments

Principal components —the dimensions of our set of revealed representations— are ordered according to how much of the variance in the original data they account for (Jolliffe, 2011).

---

[22]In terms of party self-identification we have: 43% Democrats, 27% Republicans and 30% independents. The age of our respondents ranged from 21 to 90 with a median of 41. The majority of our sample reported having a college degree (60%). 19% of our sample reported being from a minority race (including Hispanics).

[23]The use of free associations is not in itself a novel idea, see for example Szalay and Brent (1967) and Zaller and Feldman (1992), however these previous efforts made a very different use of the data.

[24]As an alternative method, we used latent semantic analysis (Landauer and Dumais, 1997). All results hold. This is not surprising given the correspondence between both methods.

They are not labeled in any meaningful way, instead it is up to the researcher to interpret them. To do so we rely on variable loadings —the set of weights by which the original variables are multiplied to make up a given component. Loadings on the first principal component will be informative of the most salient dimension —of the latent semantic space— during retrieval. According to *Hypothesis 1* this dimension should be valence. To be consistent with this, the first principal component must be evaluative in nature, that is, assign high absolute loadings to strongly valenced words, and exhibit two strongly, oppositely valenced poles. We can inspect the words with the highest loadings on the first component to visually determine whether they follow this pattern.

It is possible for more than one component to be valenced. To be able to claim the first component is 'the valence' dimension —the dimension likely to drive evaluative judgments— we also need to show it is more strongly valenced than all other components. To compute the valence of all components, we use valence norms from psychology (Warriner, Kuperman and Brysbaert, 2013). These provide valence ratings —from 1 (unhappy) to 9 (happy)— for close to 14,000 English words.[25] For each feature —listed word— we compute its standardized valence score.[26] Then for each principal component we compute its *valence intensity* as the weighted sum of these standardized valence scores, using component loadings as weights. We compare the first principal component with all other components using this measure.

To evaluate *Hypothesis 2* we use the first principal component of each cue as a predictor of attitudes towards *welfare* and *government services*. For each type of attitude —toward *welfare* and *government services*— we estimate five separate regressions, one for each principal component as a regressor. In all regressions we control for list length, age, gender, college attendance, minority status, ideological self-placement (Liberal, moderate, Conservative) and party identification (Democrat, independent, Republican).

---

[25]These are crowdsourced ratings. Participants are asked to rate words according to how they feel when reading the word.

[26]The norms dataset did not include all words in our data. On average 29% of the words listed for a given cue also appeared in the norms dataset. This ranged from 24% for `American values` and `government` to 34% for `Republican`.

2.7.2 Shared Representations

Using the set of revealed representations, we can compute the representational similarity — cosine similarity— between all pairs of subjects (dyads). We then apply K-means clustering to the set of dyad similarities for each cue and evaluate the optimal number of clusters using the average silhouette width.[27] According to *Hypothesis 3*, cluster assignments should be highly correlated given the presence of shared constraints. To evaluate this we use the cluster assignment for a given cue as a predictor of cluster assignment for another cue and repeat this for every cue pair, controlling for age, gender, college attendance, minority status, ideological self placement (Liberal, moderate, Conservative) and party identification (Democrat, independent, Republican).

2.8   Results

2.8.1   Memory Organization and Attitude Judgments

Figure 2.1 displays for each cue the proportion of principal components with <u>lower</u> valence intensity than the first principal component. For the cues `welfare`, `Republican` and `Democrat` we observe that the first principal component is the most valenced. For `American values` the first component is not the most valenced but is among the top valenced components. Only for the cue `government` do we observe that the first principal component is not at all valenced relative to the other components. We interpret these results as indicating that for `welfare`, `Republican`, `Democrat` and to a lesser degree `American values`, the valence dimension carried greater weight when retrieving words 'similar' to the cue. We can visually confirm this by looking at the loadings of the first principal component (see Figure 2.2).

---

[27]The average silhouette width is a ratio-type index comparing an observation's contribution to within cluster cohesion and across cluster separation (Arbelaitz et al., 2013; Rousseeuw, 1987).

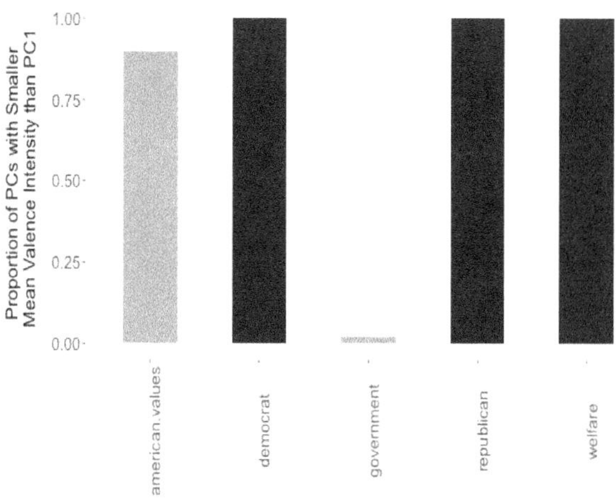

Figure 2.1: Valence Intensity of Principal Components

Table 2.2 summarizes the results of using the first principal component as a predictor of attitudes. For readability it shows only the coefficients of the first principal component regressor for each regression (see Supporting Information for full table of coefficients). In the case of attitudes toward welfare, the first principal component of the cues `welfare`, `Republican` and `Democrat` are all highly significant. Results are very similar in the case of attitudes toward government services except that the first principal component of `government` is also highly predictive.

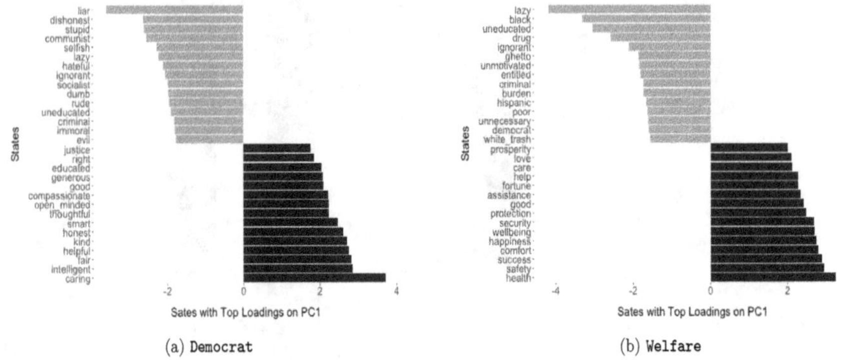

(a) **Democrat** (b) **Welfare**

Figure 2.2: Word Loadings on the First Principal Component

	welfare	government services
government	−0.010	0.054***
	(0.023)	(0.021)
American values	0.023	−0.001
	(0.025)	(0.023)
welfare	0.153***	0.180***
	(0.022)	(0.020)
Republican	0.148***	0.147***
	(0.026)	(0.022)
Democrat	0.124***	0.159***
	(0.024)	(0.024)

Notes: *p<0.1; **p<0.05; ***p<0.01

Table 2.2: First Principal Component as Predictor of Attitudes

The fact that these coefficients are significant even after controlling for ideology and party identification suggest this first dimension of our revealed representations is capturing more attitudinally relevant information than that captured by traditional Liker-type questions on political affiliation. Moreover, it is not just the components specific to the cues **welfare** and **government** that are predictive of their respective attitude questions but rather, with some exceptions, the full set of components. That is, we can draw inferences on attitudes toward government services from knowledge of how the concept `welfare` or `Democrat` are represented in memory. This is consistent with the presence of ideology-like constraints in the organization of semantic memory.

2.8.2 Shared Representations

Consistent with *Hypothesis 3*, we find all cues exhibit clusters in terms of the representational similarity between subjects. Except for the cue `Republican` for which 3 is the optimal number of clusters, all cues have 2 clusters according to this metric (see Figure 2.3). Moreover, these clusters vary in terms of average valence of their retrieved associations, suggesting they are attitudinally driven.

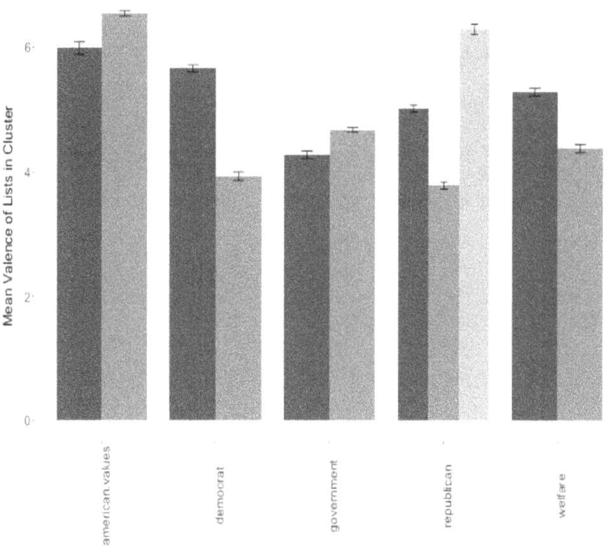

Figure 2.3: Mean Cluster Valence

Table 2.3 summarizes the regressions among the set of five cluster assignments. We find broad support for our hypothesis. Cluster assignment for a given cue is highly predictive of cluster assignment for all other cues.[28]

	government	American values	welfare	Republican	Democrat
government	1	0.22***	-0.26***	-0.16***	-0.13***
American values	.	1	-0.16***	-0.09***	-0.09*
welfare	.	.	1	0.04*	0.08*
Republican	.	.	.	1	0.30***
Democrat	.	.	.	.	1

Table 2.3: Cluster Assignment Regressions

2.9 Correspondence with Self-Identification

Consistent with our definition of ideology, the above results suggest the existence of shared constraints in memory organization that are relevant for political attitude judgments. We now turn to the question of correspondence between memory organization and other measures of ideology, namely self-reported measures. Are self-reported measures at all meaningful? We argue such self-reported measures are meaningful insofar as they capture latent differences in semantic memory organization. Below we propose two different tests to evaluate this correspondence. Both show evidence of a strong correspondence between ideological self-identification and memory organization.

2.9.1 Ideology Classifier

As a first test of this correspondence, we treat the first principal component of each revealed representation as a classifier. We subset our dataset to include only subjects that unambiguously identified themselves ideologically as being either Conservative or Liberal.[29] We next classify each subject as either Liberal or Conservative as function of the sign of their coordinate on the first principal component.[30] Figure 2.4 plots the accuracy score for each cue.

---

[28]Negative values are a result of cluster labels being assigned independently for each cue. So individuals that are in cluster 1 for welfare may be in cluster 2 for government. What matters is that subjects tend to belong to the same clusters across all concepts.

[29]This includes subjects that identified themselves as either Strongly Liberal, Liberal, Conservative or Strongly Conservative. This group represents 58% of our sample.

[30]To determine whether to classify a negative coordinate as Liberal or Conservative we use whichever assignment yields the highest accuracy.

Figure 2.4: First Principal Component as a Classifier of Ideology

As baselines we use both an 'all same-class' classifier —the dotted line at 0.5— and accuracy scores for gender.[31] Simply using this first component we can achieve high accuracy scores for the set of cues we found to have the most valenced first principal component: `Democrat`, `Republican` and `welfare`. Plotting each subject according to their coordinates on the first two principal components visually confirms this result (see Figure 2.5). This is not the case when we classify by gender.

2.9.2 Correlates of Representationl Similarity

Using regression analysis we evaluate the correlates of the computed dyad similarity scores. As regressors we use dyad-specific covariates including: the minimum list length of the two lists (`min.num.words`), the age difference between i and j (`age.dist`), whether i and j share the same gender (`same.gender`), whether both are white or from a minority group (`same.minority`), whether both did not attend college (`both.nocollege`), whether both

---

[31]We adjust accuracy scores for class imbalance.

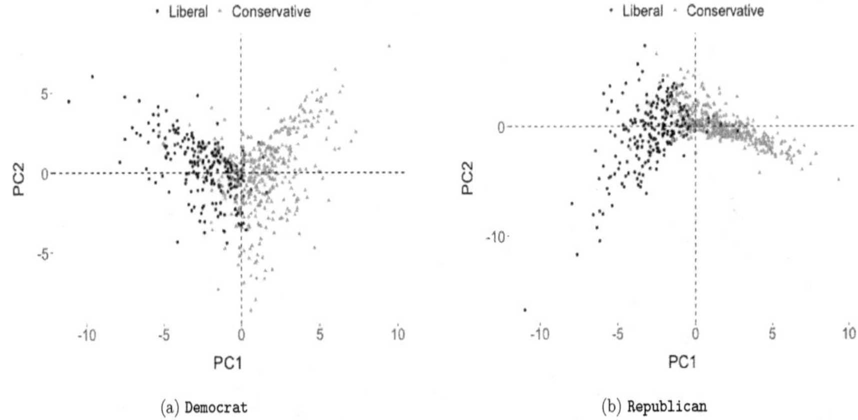

Figure 2.5: Subject Coordinates on the First Two Principal Components

attended college (`both.college`) and ideological distance (`ideology.dist`).[32] In addition we included the interaction between the college and no-college indicators and ideological distance. Previous research, beginning with Converse (1962), suggests that ideological constraints are less common among low-education voters.[33] This would result in a weaker correspondence between ideological self-identification and memory organization for subjects with no college education.

It is clear that the independence assumption required for OLS does not hold for dyadic data —the same subject appears in multiple dyads. Failing to account for this dependence will result in mistaken inferences as the standard errors are likely to be underestimated. To adjust the standard errors we apply the non-parametric standard error adjustment proposed by (Aronow, Samii and Assenova, 2015). Figure 2.6 displays the resulting coefficients for each cue word. Gender, education, minority status and ideology all appear to be correlated with representational similarity with coefficients signed in the expected direction, that is, dyads with common values in these variables tend to have more similar representations. In the case of ideology we again observe differences between cues, with the `welfare`, `Republican`

---

[32]Ideological distance is computed using a 7-item Likert-type question on ideological self-identification.

[33]This is also consistent with research suggesting more educated voters often hold more polarized views (Drummond and Fischhoff, 2017).

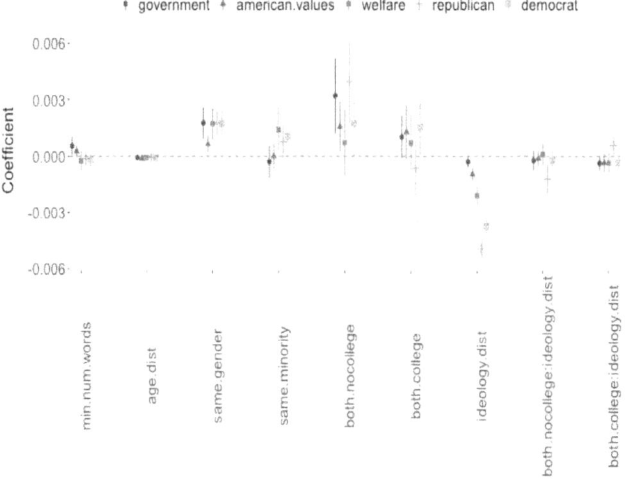

Figure 2.6: Correlates of Representational Similarity

and `Democrat` showing the largest effects. The interaction effects yield mixed results, in some cases —`government` and `American values`— indicating that college potentiates the effect of ideological distance while in others —`Republican`— there seems to be a dampening effect. Interestingly, minority status shows the largest effects for `welfare` and `Democrat`, a result that is arguably consistent with *welfare* being a particularly relevant political issue for minorities (see Supporting Information for full regression table).

These results confirm a correspondence between memory organization and self-declared ideology. Survey questions on ideology and attitudes more broadly are clearly, indeed almost by necessity, capturing differences in memory structures. However, these are only snapshots of a much bigger picture, as evidenced by our attitude regressions —i.e. the first principal components remain significant even after controlling for these traditionally highly predictive variables.

2.10 Discussion

In this paper we made the case for an approach to the study of ideology centered on memory organization. Starting with the premise that voters' attitudes are a reflection of how their semantic memory is organized we argued ideology should be understood as *shared constraints on the organization of political concepts in semantic memory*. With this definition in hand, we derive multiple hypotheses along with the requisite methods to evaluate them. Our results broadly support the presence of shared constraints in the organization of political concepts in semantic memory, a result that contrasts with a significant chunk of the literature on ideology, beginning with Converse's seminal work (Converse, 1962). Moreover, results from the attitude regressions (see Table 2.2) indicate our memory based measure —the first principal component of our set of revealed representations— is capturing more attitudinally relevant information than traditionally highly predictive variables (party and ideological self-identification). Finally, we also provided evidence of a correspondence between memory organization and self-reported ideology. Nevertheless, to make any definitive claims requires we apply this protocol to a broader set of concepts and, importantly, explore stability over time and in different contexts. Moreover, the strength of our results varied by concept. This is perhaps unsurprising as some concepts are clearly more polarizing than others (e.g. party names) and some concepts were potentially too abstract (e.g. government). Overall, this paper serves to highlight the potential value added of approaching the study of ideology and attitudes more broadly from a cognitive, memory-centered perspective.

Supporting Information for Chapter 2

B.1: Semantic Fluency Task Wording

In what follows you will be asked to complete 5 word association tasks. <u>For each one</u>:

- You will be given a category label.

- You will have 2 minutes to <u>list words</u> you associate with the given category.

- Try to <u>list as many distinct words as you can</u> in the time given.

- Try to <u>write continuously</u>, listing words as they come to mind.

- <u>Do not repeat words within a category label</u>.

- You may repeat words across category labels if considered relevant.

- The next category label will appear automatically after the 2 minutes are up.

>>

Figure 2.7: Semantic Fluency Task Wording

B.2: Attitude Questions

Some people think the government should provide fewer services even in areas such as health and education in order to reduce spending. Suppose these people are at one end of a scale, at point 1. Other people feel it is important for the government to provide many more services even if it means an increase in spending. Suppose these people are at the other end, at point 7. And, of course, some other people have opinions somewhere in between, at points 2, 3, 4, 5 or 6.

Where would you place yourself on this scale, or haven't you thought much about this?

  1. Government should provide many fewer services

  2.

  3.

  4.

  5.

  6.

  7. Government should provide many more services

  Haven't thought much about this

(a) `Government Services`

Some people feel the government in Washington should see to it that every person has a job and a good standard of living. Suppose these people are at one end of a scale, at point 1. Others think the government should just let each person get ahead on their own. Suppose these people are at the other end, at point 7. And, of course, some other people have opinions somewhere in between, at points 2, 3, 4, 5, or 6.

Where would you place yourself on this scale, or haven't you thought much about this?

  1. Government should see to jobs and standard of living

  2.

  3.

  4.

  5.

  6.

  7. Government should let each person get ahead on their own

  Haven't thought much about this

(b) `Welfare`

Figure 2.8: Attitudinal Questions

B.3: Attitude Regressions

	Dependent variable: attitudes toward expanding welfare				
	government	American Values	Welfare	Republican	Democrat
List length	−0.0004	−0.028**	0.026**	0.008	−0.008
	(0.014)	(0.014)	(0.012)	(0.013)	(0.013)
Age (years)	−0.002	−0.003	−0.001	−0.003	−0.003
	(0.004)	(0.004)	(0.004)	(0.004)	(0.004)
Gender (male = 1)	−0.248**	−0.263***	−0.203**	−0.247**	−0.200**
	(0.101)	(0.101)	(0.099)	(0.099)	(0.100)
College (attended = 1)	−0.221**	−0.201**	−0.205**	−0.231**	−0.244**
	(0.102)	(0.102)	(0.099)	(0.099)	(0.100)
Minority status (white = 1)	−0.190	−0.162	−0.207	−0.194	−0.142
	(0.133)	(0.132)	(0.129)	(0.130)	(0.131)
PC1	−0.010	0.023	0.153***	0.148***	0.124***
	(0.023)	(0.025)	(0.022)	(0.024)	(0.026)
Ideology (Liberal = 1)	2.235***	2.189***	2.101***	1.815***	1.975***
	(0.203)	(0.204)	(0.199)	(0.212)	(0.207)
Ideology (moderate = 1)	0.943***	0.877***	0.911***	0.719***	0.749***
	(0.163)	(0.164)	(0.159)	(0.164)	(0.165)
Party (independent = 1)	−0.342**	−0.356**	−0.278**	−0.266*	−0.169
	(0.140)	(0.140)	(0.136)	(0.137)	(0.143)
Party (Republican = 1)	−0.812***	−0.837***	−0.587***	−0.507***	−0.548***
	(0.189)	(0.188)	(0.185)	(0.190)	(0.196)
Constant	3.775***	4.077***	3.444***	3.869***	3.855***
	(0.317)	(0.322)	(0.305)	(0.317)	(0.308)
Observations	952	951	948	952	952
R^2	0.371	0.380	0.406	0.396	0.391
Adjusted R^2	0.365	0.374	0.400	0.390	0.384

Notes: *p<0.1; **p<0.05; ***p<0.01.
Higher values of the dependent variable mean more 'Liberal' attitudes.
Baseline category for ideology is 'Conservative'. Baseline category for party is 'Democrat'.

	Dependent variable: attitudes toward expanding government services				
	government	American Values	Welfare	Republican	Democrat
List length	−0.036***	−0.036***	−0.001	−0.017	−0.036***
	(0.012)	(0.013)	(0.011)	(0.012)	(0.012)
Age (years)	−0.006*	−0.006*	−0.005	−0.007**	−0.007**
	(0.003)	(0.003)	(0.003)	(0.003)	(0.003)
Gender (male = 1)	−0.102	−0.123	−0.090	−0.128	−0.061
	(0.092)	(0.092)	(0.089)	(0.090)	(0.090)
College (attended = 1)	−0.256***	−0.241***	−0.217**	−0.250***	−0.257***
	(0.093)	(0.093)	(0.089)	(0.090)	(0.090)
Minority status (white = 1)	−0.150	−0.159	−0.217*	−0.166	−0.129
	(0.120)	(0.120)	(0.115)	(0.117)	(0.117)
PC1	0.054***	−0.001	0.180***	0.147***	0.159***
	(0.021)	(0.023)	(0.020)	(0.022)	(0.024)
Ideology (Liberal = 1)	2.350***	2.253***	2.176***	1.932***	2.004***
	(0.185)	(0.186)	(0.178)	(0.192)	(0.186)
Ideology (moderate = 1)	1.102***	1.008***	1.023***	0.835***	0.824***
	(0.149)	(0.149)	(0.143)	(0.149)	(0.149)
Party (independent = 1)	−0.415***	−0.466***	−0.373***	−0.350***	−0.228*
	(0.127)	(0.127)	(0.121)	(0.125)	(0.129)
Party (Republican = 1)	−0.982***	−1.038***	−0.788***	−0.705***	−0.678***
	(0.171)	(0.171)	(0.165)	(0.172)	(0.176)
Constant	4.480***	4.592***	4.147***	4.529***	4.549***
	(0.289)	(0.293)	(0.273)	(0.289)	(0.278)
Observations	955	954	950	955	955
R^2	0.456	0.460	0.502	0.476	0.483

Notes: *p<0.1; **p<0.05; ***p<0.01.
Higher values of the dependent variable mean more 'Liberal' attitudes.
Baseline category for ideology is 'Conservative'. Baseline category for party is 'Democrat'.

B.4: Dyadic Regressions

	Dependent variable: dyad cosine similarity				
	government	American Values	Welfare	Republican	Democrat
Min. # of words	0.001**	0.0003**	−0.0002	−0.0002	−0.0002
	(0.0003)	(0.0002)	(0.0003)	(0.0002)	(0.0002)
Age difference	−0.0001***	−0.0001***	−0.0001***	−0.0001***	−0.0001***
	(0.00001)	(0.00002)	(0.00002)	(0.00002)	(0.00002)
Gender (same = 1)	0.002***	0.001***	0.002***	0.002***	0.002***
	(0.0004)	(0.0002)	(0.0004)	(0.0003)	(0.0003)
Minority status (same = 1)	−0.0003	−0.00000	0.0014**	0.0007**	0.0010***
	(0.0004)	(0.0003)	(0.0006)	(0.0004)	(0.0004)
No-college (same = 1)	0.003***	0.002**	0.001	0.004***	0.002**
	(0.0010)	(0.0007)	(0.0009)	(0.0011)	(0.0009)
College (same = 1)	0.001**	0.001**	0.001	−0.001	0.002**
	(0.0006)	(0.0007)	(0.0007)	(0.0007)	(0.0008)
Ideology distance	−0.0003***	−0.001***	−0.002***	−0.005***	−0.004***
	(0.0002)	(0.0002)	(0.0003)	(0.0003)	(0.0003)
No-college*Ideology distance	−0.0002	−0.0001	0.0001	−0.001***	−0.0002
	(0.0003)	(0.0002)	(0.0003)	(0.0004)	(0.0003)
College*Ideology distance	−0.0004**	−0.0004*	−0.0003	0.001**	−0.0003
	(0.0002)	(0.0003)	(0.0003)	(0.0003)	(0.0002)
Constant	−0.003	0.002	0.007***	0.011***	0.009***
	(0.0022)	(0.001)	(0.0022)	(0.0015)	(0.0015)
Observations	538,203	537,166	530,965	538,203	538,203
R^2	0.001	0.001	0.002	0.013	0.009
Adjusted R^2	0.001	0.001	0.002	0.013	0.009

Notes: *p<0.1; **p<0.05; ***p<0.01.

Chapter 3

Word Embeddings: A Framework for Model Comparison and Validation

3.1 Introduction

Word embeddings are all the buzz in the distributional semantics block. Word embeddings 'embed' words —discrete symbols to begin with— in a multidimensional space wherein distance between words is informative of semantic similarity. These models have seen tremendous success in a variety of tasks, most notably as feature representations in downstream NLP tasks such as parts-of-speech tagging, named-entity-recognition, sentiment analysis and document retrieval. Now word embeddings are rapidly making their way into the social sciences, political science being no exception. However, as is often the case with technology transfers, adoption seems likely to outpace understanding. In this paper we set out to pre-empt this outcome.

Broadly speaking word embeddings serve two functions: (1) as feature representations for downstream NLP tasks and (2) to study word usage and meaning —semantics. Good performance in the former need not, indeed often does not, correlate with good performance in the latter (Chiu, Korhonen and Pyysalo, 2016). In this paper we focus on the use of embeddings to study meaning. We do so for several reasons: first, downstream tasks tend to be supervised in which case validation is arguably straightforward and specific to the task at hand. Moreover, supervised tasks are not all too common in political science (Denny and Spirling, 2018). Second, the study of meaning, including differences between groups and changes over time, is of obvious interest to political scientists. For this purpose, existing validation metrics from the computational linguistics literature —e.g. word similarity tasks using datasets of human similarity ratings from psychology— are unlikely to capture the semantics specific to political texts and indeed have important limitations in their own right (Faruqui et al., 2016).

With this in mind we lay out a framework to evaluate embedding models along both technical and substantive criteria. We apply this framework to a set of corpora varying in size and language (English, Spanish and German). While we must necessarily restrict the number of models and parameters we evaluate, we stress that the work-flow outlined in this paper can easily be adapted to evaluate new models —including non-embedding models of semantics— and other parameter variations. Overall our results show embeddings capture political semantics remarkably well, with a novel Turing-style metric showing embeddings approaching, and in some cases surpassing, human performance in the generation of semantically meaningful associations to words. Moreover, political scientists will find comfort in the result that easily available pre-trained embeddings capture well the semantics of political texts, as suggested by strong correlations with a broad set of more laborious locally trained models. Along with an intuitive workflow for model comparison and validation, we offer practitioners a series of main takeaways drawn from training hundreds of embedding models and performing thousands of human validations.

Political scientists are rightly attracted to the potential of word embeddings. It is our hope with this paper to provide them with a series of tools and the basic understanding necessary to easily and in an informed manner apply them to their research. Before laying out our approach we begin with a brief history of how embedding models originated followed by an account of the more popular models.

3.2   Word Embeddings: A Brief History

Word embedding models are the newest members of a family of models known interchangeably as distributional semantic models (DSMs) —our preferred label— semantic vector space models or word space models. The basic premise underlying DSMs is that a word's contextual information —quantified as co-occurrence statistics— provides a basis for its semantic representation, an idea dating back to the 1950s (Firth, 1957*b*; Harris, 1954; Wittgenstein, 1953) and later formalized in the form of the *distributional hypothesis* (Harris, 1970). Intuitively, the distributional hypothesis posits that words that appear in similar contexts are likely to be semantically proximate. It would take several decades for the distributional hypothesis to be tested at scale with the emergence of models —DSMs— trained on large corpora. Notable mentions include Latent Semantic Analysis (Landauer and Dumais, 1997), Hyperspace Analogue to Language (HAL) (Lund and Burgess, 1996*a*), Latent Dirichlet Allocation (LDA) (Blei, Ng and Jordan, 2003) and the Bound Encoding of the Aggregate Language Environment (BEAGLE) (Jones, Kintsch and Mewhort, 2006). All these models can trace their origin to either the information retrieval or cognitive modeling literatures.

Despite sharing a common theoretical support —the distributional hypothesis— word embeddings have an altogether different origin in the computational linguistics literature. The objective in language models is to maximize the conditional probability of the next word given N previous words. This requires modeling the joint distribution of words, a rather difficult endeavor if we treat words as discrete atomic symbols.[1] Bengio et al. (2003) proposed modeling words as distributed representations within a neural language model that simultaneously learns the *word feature vectors* —the word embeddings— and the parameters

---

[1] For one, discrete atomic symbols capture no information on the semantic similarity between different terms, **cat** and **dog** are equally distinct as **cat** and **train**. This greatly limits the model's ability to generalize beyond sequences of words observed in the training set. From a computational standpoint, as the vocabulary grows we quickly run into the curse of dimensionality and the resulting data sparsity, requiring increasing amounts of data for training.

of the probabilistic language model.[2] Notice that 'context' in these models is defined locally —the previous N words— rather than at the level of the document.[3] This is a first key difference between embedding models and the DSMs most political scientists will be familiar with.

Building on this work, (Collobert and Weston, 2008; Collobert et al., 2011) were the first to demonstrate that word embeddings carry syntactic and semantic meaning and showcased their value as features in a broad set of downstream NLP tasks beyond language modeling, including parts-of-speech tagging, chunking and named entity recognition among others.[4] However, it was not until the release of Word2Vec that word embeddings began to be widely adopted (Mikolov, Chen, Corrado and Dean, 2013). In Bengio et al. (2003) and Collobert and Weston (2008) word embeddings were features inside a larger neural network model. In contrast, Word2Vec's objective is to produce accurate word representations evaluated using a series of intrinsic tasks (e.g. word similarity and analogy tasks). Unhindered by additional modeling constraints, Mikolov, Chen, Corrado and Dean (2013) proposed several innovations that greatly reduced the complexity of the model and allowed for its scaling to huge corpora and vocabularies.[5] Soon after the release of Word2Vec, Pennington, Socher and Manning (2014) proposed a competing algorithm —GloVe— that showed improved performance in a number of tasks. A key contributing factor to the meteorite rise of word embeddings was the release of specialized software that allowed researchers to use pre-trained embeddings or estimate their own at relatively low computational cost.

---

[2]The idea of using distributed representations for symbolic data was not new (Elman, 1990; Hinton, McClelland, Rumelhart et al., 1986; Paccanaro and Hinton, 2000; Rumelhart, Hinton and Williams, 1986), Bengio et al's innovation was in bringing together various technologies for its scalable application in language modeling.

[3]Current embedding models all use symmetric windows around the target word.

[4]Notably, they also proposed modifying the objective function to distinguish between correct and incorrect word sequences rather than predict the next word. This greatly alleviated one of the computational bottlenecks of Bengio et al's model —the computation of the softmax in the final layer of the network— and was a precursor to Mikolov et al's negative sampling method Mikolov, Sutskever, Chen, Corrado and Dean (2013).

[5]These included the elimination of the non-linear transformation and the resulting hidden layer common to both Bengio et al. (2003) and Collobert and Weston (2008), the use of symmetric context windows and estimation using negative sampling. Word2Vec also included several pre-processing steps that are key to its performance (Levy, Goldberg and Dagan, 2015).

3.3 Word Embeddings Explained

In this section we briefly walk the reader through the three 'original' and still popular word embedding models, Word2Vec's two variants, CBOW and Skip-Gram, along with Pennington et al's GloVe. All subsequent models are in one way or another variations of these — mostly of Word2Vec (see for example FastText Joulin et al. (2016)). We begin with Word2Vec.

3.3.1 Word2Vec

Neural networks consist of the following ingredients: input data and corresponding targets, a set of connected layers that transform inputs into outputs —these make up the network— a loss function —quantifies the algorithm's performance— and an optimizer —a way for the model to update parameters based on the signal provided by the loss function. The goal is to 'learn' increasingly meaningful representations of the inputs to arrive at the expected outputs. Let's begin with the inputs and targets.

For readers familiar with machine learning, the mention of inputs and targets should bring to mind supervised learning. But where does the labeled data to learn word representations come from? Word2Vec generates its own 'labeled' data by moving a local window of a given size —a hyperparameter defined by the user— from word to word in the corpus.[6] Take the following sentence from Douglas Adam's Hitchhiker's Guide to the Galaxy:

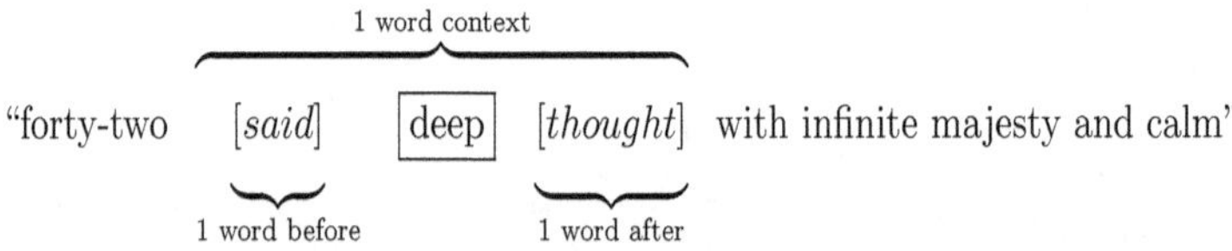

Using a symmetric window size of 1 we get the following input target pairs: [forty-two, said], [said, forty-two] [said, deep], [deep, said], [deep, thought], [thought, deep],

---

[6]Word embeddings are unsupervised in the sense that the they do not require human-annotated data. However, they are trained as a supervised model on their own self-annotated data.

[thought, with], [with, thought], [with, infinite], [infinite, with], [infinite, majesty], [majesty, infinite], [majesty, and], [and, majesty], [and, calm], [calm, and]. Each of these pairs consists of a focus word and a context word. Which we define as the input and which as the target determines what architecture of Word2Vec we are using. In the Continuous Bag of Words (CBOW) model, the focus word (the target) is predicted from the set of context words (the input). The Skip-Gram model, on the other hand, is trained to predict the set of context words (the targets) given the focus word (the input).[7] Given inputs and corresponding targets we now turn to the network model.

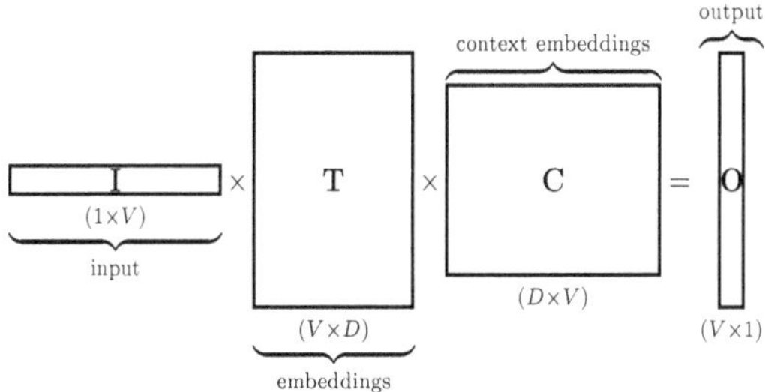

Figure 3.1: Skip-Gram Architecture

Denote V as the number of words in the corpus vocabulary. The model includes two weight matrices, one of dimensions $V \times D$ and another of dimensions $D \times V$ (see Figure 3.1). The parameter D, the *embedding dimensions*, is a user-defined hyperparameter specifying the number of 'neurons' in the hidden layer and, ultimately, the dimensions of the embedding space.[8] These weight matrices are the model's trainable parameters, those that will be adjusted as the model 'learns'. The setup in Figure 3.1 is the Skip-Gram architecture.[9] Note, each word in the vocabulary has a corresponding representation in each matrix —a representation as a focus word in the embeddings matrix and a representation as a context word in the context embeddings matrix.[10] Initially both matrices are filled

---

[7]In contrast to traditional DSMs for which the vocabulary is often heavily pre-processed —removal of punctuation, removal of stopwords and numbers, stemming etc.— there is relatively little pre-processing of the vocabulary prior to fitting word embedding models. Most often punctuation is removed, numbers are replaced with a single token (e.g. *num*) and words are lower cased. It is also common to restrict the vocabulary using a minimum count threshold —usually 5 to 10.

[8]The hidden layer refers to the vector resulting from multiplying the input vector and the embeddings matrix.

[9]In the CBOW architecture, the first of these matrices corresponds to the *context embeddings* and the second to the *embeddings*.

[10]Usually the context embeddings are discarded at the end, although some authors suggest using the addition of the two as

with small randomly initialized values. These values are subsequently adjusted as the model iterates over input-target pairs. The steps for a single input-target pair are as follows: draw an input-target pair, *pass* the input *forward* through the network, obtain a prediction for the target, compare the prediction to the true target and compute a loss, update weights —both target and context embeddings— such that loss is reduced for the given input-target pair. Let's look at what is going on underneath the hood along each of these steps. We will repeatedly refer to the dimensions of the different components as it helps with the intuition.

Suppose our focus-context pair is [deep, thought]. We want our model to predict the context word thought given the focus word deep. We "feed" the model the word deep as a one-hot encoding or one-hot vector representation. For each word in our vocabulary, it's one-hot coded representation consists of a vector of size $1 \times V$ with all entries set to zero except for the i th entry —i being a unique integer index associated to the word — which is set to 1. This index also corresponds to the <u>row</u> in the embeddings matrix and the <u>column</u> in the context embeddings matrix corresponding to each word's representations.

The one-hot vector of deep is multiplied with the embeddings matrix —of dimensions $V \times D$— resulting in a hidden layer vector of dimensions $1 \times D$. All that has happened in this step is that the model has "selected" the embedding for our focus word deep.[11] The resulting $1 \times D$ vector is then multiplied with the context embeddings matrix —of dimensions $D \times V$— resulting in a $1 \times V$ output vector. Each entry of this vector corresponds to the dot product of the embedding and the context embedding of a word in the vocabulary. These values are a measure of distance in the D-dimensional embedding space between the focus word and all words in the vocabulary. We normalize the output vector using a softmax function —exponentiate each value and divide by the vector sum— resulting in a vector of probabilities which sum to 1.[12] This output vector is our model's prediction.

---

the final embeddings (Pennington, Socher and Manning, 2014).

[11]In neural network terminology we say the activation function for the hidden layer is linear. This aspect of Word2Vec contrasts with most other neural networks in which the activation function is non-linear, allowing for increasingly complex transformations of the input data.

[12]It is common to use logs in this step, transforming the division into a subtraction of log-sum of exponentiated values.

To evaluate how our model performed we must compare this output to the expected output, namely the one-hot encoded vector of the target word **thought**. If our model performed well, all values of the output vector will be close to 0 except for the index corresponding to the target word which should be close to 1 —that is, the target word should have a high probability assigned to it. Notice the probability will be a function of how close the two words are on the embedding space —recall it originates from the dot product. Now we just need a loss function to generate a summary statistic of our model's performance based on the difference between the predicted output and the target. A popular choice is the cross-entropy loss function. Model loss will be larger the larger the distance between the input **deep** and the target **thought**. Adjusting parameters will require moving the embeddings —and context embeddings— in a way that brings input and target words closer together in the embedding space. As in all optimization methods with differentiable objective functions, neural networks are optimized using the gradient —the direction of greatest change— of the loss function with respect to the model's parameters. In neural networks the gradient is computed using *backward propagation* which is little more than applying the chain rule beginning at the end of the network.

3.3.2 GloVe

Word2Vec follows an *online learning* approach —the model is trained as the context window is moved from word to word along the corpus. The model at no point sees the global co-occurrence counts of any pairs of words in the vocabulary. This setup may seem odd to readers acquainted with traditional DSMs for which a matrix of global co-occurrence counts —either in the form of a document-term matrix or a term-term matrix— serves as the starting point. In motivating Global Vectors —GloVe for short— Pennington, Socher and Manning (2014) argue that in failing to use global co-occurrence counts Word2Vec makes poor use of corpus statistics for learning meaningful word representations. On the other hand, DSMs utilizing global co-occurrence counts followed by some form of matrix factorization (e.g.

Probability and Ratio	k=representative	k= senator	k=lower	k=upper	k=legal	k=wheel
$P(k|congress)$	1.446×10^{-04}	0.001	5.846×10^{-05}	8.224×10^{-06}	0.0001	2.324×10^{-06}
$P(k|senate)$	4.343×10^{-05}	0.002	3.100×10^{-05}	9.467×10^{-06}	0.0001	2.413×10^{-06}
$P(k|congress)/P(k|senate)$	3.330	0.201	1.886	0.869	1.001	0.963

Table 3.1: Co-occurrence probabilities
Note: Estimates based on our Congressional Records corpus.

LSA) lack the meaningful linear properties that have become associated with embeddings — e.g. `king` - `man` + `woman` = `queen`. This, they argue, suggests a sub-optimal mapping onto a common low-dimensional vector-space. As an alternative, they propose a middle of the road approach in which word embeddings are learned by iteratively approximating the product of all possible word-pairs in the corpus vocabulary to their respective global co-occurrence count. The counts in GloVe are based on local window contexts —the size of which is a user-defined hyperparameter as in Word2Vec— not document level counts.

A key insight underpinning GloVe's objective function is that ratios of co-occurrence probabilities are more informative —in terms of semantics— than are co-occurrence probabilities per se. Suppose we are interested in exploring the relationship between the words `congress` and `senate`. One alternative is to look at their co-occurrence probabilities with other words (the first two rows of Table 3.1). These reveal `senator` is the term most proximate to `congress` and `senate` from the set of probe words. Alternatively we can study the ratios of co-occurrence probabilities. We expect higher ratios (> 1) for words more semantically proximate to `congress` than to `senate`, smaller ratios for words more semantically proximate to `senate` than to `congress` and a ratio close to 1 for words that are not useful in discriminating between the two —either because they are related to neither (`wheel`) or similarly related to both (`legal`). We immediately notice that the ratios are better able to rank the set of probe words in terms of how useful they are in discriminating between the two terms of interest. This intuition provides the starting point from which GloVe's objective function is derived.

Despite the apparent differences in the objective functions, GloVe and Word2Vec are mathematically very similar as shown by Pennington, Socher and Manning (2014). This should not be all that surprising since the number of times Word2Vec will observe a given training pair once the moving window has covered the entire corpus is exactly equal to the total co-occurrence count used in GloVe's objective function.

3.4   Embedding Models and Parameter Choices

The application of any statistical model requires choices; embeddings are no exception. For political scientists downloading code (or indeed downloading pre-fit embeddings), at the very least, they need to decide:

1. how large a **window size** they want the model to use.

2. how large an **embedding** they wish to use to represent their words.

3. whether to fit the embedding models **locally**, or to use **pre-trained** embeddings fit to some other (hopefully related) corpus.

We now discuss the nature of these choices. In addition, we explain some other important features of embeddings for researchers: namely, the fact that embeddings demonstrate *instability* in practice, and what one might do about this. In general, we note that there is often little guidance in the literature as to how decisions should be made—and virtually none at all for social science problems. A final caveat here is that, of course, there are many other parameter choices beyond the ones we specify in this section; for example, `Word2Vec` allows one to choose a learning rate for its backpropagation algorithm, and all models can use documents that have been pre-processed differently. Using our methods below, users can make decisions over them in the same way. But we keep our focus on the three above because they seem most central to empirical research.

3.4.1 Window-size

Window-size determines the number of words, on either side of the focus word to be included in its context.[13] The type of semantic relationship captured by embeddings has been found to vary with window-size, with larger window sizes (> 2) capturing more topical relations (e.g. `Obama` - `President`) and smaller window sizes (< 2) capturing syntactic relations (e.g. `dance` - `dancing`).

For topical relationships, larger windows (usually 5 or above) tend to produce better quality embeddings although with decreasing returns—a result highlighted by Mikolov, Chen, Corrado and Dean (2013) and which we corroborate below. Intuitively, larger contexts provide more information to discriminate between different words.[14] Take, for example, the following two sentences: `cows eat grass` and `lions eat meat`. A window-size of 1 does not provide enough information to distinguish between `cows` and `lions` (we know they both `eat`, but we don't know what) whereas a window-size of 2 does.

3.4.2 Embedding Dimensions

This parameter determines the dimensions of the embedding vectors which usually range between $50 - 450$. We can think of these dimensions as capturing different aspects of "meaning" or semantics that can be used to organize words.[15] Too few dimensions—imagine the extreme of 1—and there can be no meaningful separability of words; too many, and some dimensions are likely to be redundant (go unused). Factors such as vocabulary size and topical specificity of the corpus are likely to play a role, although theoretical work in this area remains scant.[16] Empirically, more dimensions generally improve performance across a

---

[13]Context windows can also be asymmetric, in which case window-size refers to the number of words on one side of the focus word to be included in its context. Asymmetric windows are better able to account for word order which may be useful for some tasks. Pennington, Socher and Manning (2014) for example find asymmetric windows to produced embeddings better suited for syntactic tasks. Nevertheless, symmetric windows are the default option for most use cases.

[14]See Supporting Information for a quick empirical verification of this claim for real data.

[15]Thinking of "meaning" in terms of dimensions in Euclidean space dates back at least to Osgood, 1952.

[16]Of the few that we could find, Patel and Bhattacharyya (2017) posit that the number of pairwise equidistant words of the corpus vocabulary measured using the term co-occurrence matrix provides a lower bound on the number of dimensions. It is not entirely clear what this equidistant metric means substantively.

wide variety of tasks but with diminishing returns. Interestingly, extant literature suggests that the point at which improvements become marginal differs depending on the problem. For downstream tasks optimal performance can sometimes be reached with as few as 50 dimensions (Melamud et al., 2016). Semantic tasks, on the other hand, continue to show significant improvements until around $200 - 300$ dimensions after which improvements are marginal (Pennington, Socher and Manning, 2014).[17] This difference is likely a result of downstream tasks leveraging specific aspects of meaning—for example, a sentiment classification task will likely benefit from embeddings that focus on discriminating words along affect-related dimensions.

3.4.3 Pre-trained Versus Going Local

Embedding models can be data hungry, meaning they need a lot of data to produce 'useful' results. Consequently, researchers with small corpora often use pre-trained embeddings. This also avoids the overhead cost associated with estimating and tuning new embeddings for each task. However, there are trade-offs. Pre-trained embeddings need not capture well the semantics of domain-specific texts. Intuitively, we want to use embeddings estimated using a corpus generated by a similar "language model" to that which generated our corpus of interest. The more similar the two language models, the more similar the underlying semantics. For a highly specific corpus—a corpus in Old English for example—it may make sense to train a local model.

Li et al. (2017) compare the performance of embeddings trained on different corpora for Twitter sentiment analysis. They find that embeddings trained on the Google News corpus perform worse—measured in terms of accuracy—than embeddings trained on Twitter data. This motivates an argument that twitter data is different. However, they also find that embeddings trained on Google News *and* Twitter data perform the best. This suggests more information is better. On the other hand, Diaz, Mitra and Craswell (2016) find

---

[17]It turns out 300 was also found to be the optimal number of dimensions in LSA (Landauer and Dumais, 1997).

that specialized embeddings—trained on a relevant subset of documents—outperform global embeddings in information retrieval tasks.[18]

An alternative to training locally is to "retrofit" global (pre-trained) embeddings to include additional information. Faruqui et al. (2014) retrofit pre-trained vectors using existing semantic lexicons such as WordNet, FrameNet, and the Paraphrase Database. They find this additional information improves performance in the standard lexical evaluation tasks. Retrofitting can also be task-specific. Kiela, Hill and Clark (2015) retrofit pre-trained embeddings to improve performance in *similarity* and *relatedness* tasks—two different tasks—using an online thesaurus and lists of free association norms for each task respectively.[19] Similarly, Yu et al. (2017) specialize word embeddings to perform sentiment analysis by retrofitting pre-trained embeddings using lists of valence norms. One final alternative is to initialize locally-trained models with pre-trained embeddings, relaxing data constraints. Again, this only makes sense if the underlying language models are not too dissimilar.

In this paper we compare the set of embeddings from a set of locally trained models using a political corpus to one of the more popular pre-trained embeddings available—GloVe. Our results show high correlations between both models, suggesting pre-trained embeddings may be appropriate for certain political corpora. However, we stress that researchers need be conscious and transparent regarding the implied assumptions when deciding to use pre-trained embeddings.

3.4.4 Instability

Word embeddings are known to be unstable (Wendlandt, Kummerfeld and Mihalcea, 2018). That is, the embedding space of two models trained on the same corpus and with the same parameter choices may differ substantially—a fact we will observe empirically below. This instability can be particularly problematic when drawing qualitative inferences from the

---

[18] The superiority of using specialized versus global information has been well established in the information retrieval literature (Attar and Fraenkel, 1977; Hull, 1994; Xu and Croft, 1996).

[19] Kiela, Hill and Clark (2015) also evaluate joint-learning models in which embeddings are estimated using both the corpus and the additional semantic lexicons. They do not find a significant performance difference compared to retrofitting.

embeddings themselves, with equivalent models producing widely different nearest neighbor rankings. Underlying this instability are various sources of randomness in the estimation of word embeddings, most notably random initialization of the embedding vectors and random order of training documents. While all words are affected, some are more affected than others (Pierrejean and Tanguy, 2018; Wendlandt, Kummerfeld and Mihalcea, 2018). It is worth noting that `GloVe` has been found to be more stable than `Word2Vec`, probably because of its use of a global co-occurrence matrix rather than an online local window context (Mimno and Thompson, 2017; Wendlandt, Kummerfeld and Mihalcea, 2018).[20]

To account for the inherent instability in the estimation process we recommend researchers estimate a given model over *multiple initializations* of the corpus—we use ten—and use the average of the similarity metric of interest. We accept that variation between realized embeddings is simply a fact of life; nonetheless, for what follows we presume that researchers want to know how stability correlates with model specification.

3.5 Evaluating Embedding Models for Social Science

As noted above, researchers face as least three "big" choices when producing word embeddings. To evaluate which choices are optimal we need evaluation tasks. For word embeddings tasks fall into one of two categories: *extrinsic* and *intrinsic*.[21] These correspond to the two main use cases of embeddings: as feature inputs and as models of semantics. Recall that our focus in this paper is on the second case.

Extrinsic tasks include various downstream NLP problems such as parts-of-speech tagging, named-entity-recognition, sentiment analysis and document retrieval. These are usually supervised, and have well-defined performance metrics. For this paper we considered evaluating embeddings this way. However, it was not immediately obvious to us which tasks,

---

[20]Separate to instability, it is reasonable to expect embeddings to differ as a result of *sampling variability*. If we view any given corpus as a particular instantiation of a superpopulation of linguistic entities, then we should adjust for this with the equivalent of a standard error. See Antoniak and Mimno (2018) for bootstrapping ideas pertaining to this problem.

[21]It is worth noting that performance in intrinsic tasks need not translate into good performance in extrinsic tasks (Chiu, Korhonen and Pyysalo, 2016).

if any, represented good baselines for political scientists.[22] As noted by Denny and Spirling (2018), there has been very low take up of supervised learning problems in political science relative to unsupervised learning problems. Moreover, as noted above, evidence of good performance need not generalize. How much should a researcher in IR update when informed that a given embedding model performs well in a classification task of congressional speeches? Given a well-defined downstream task, we recommend users first consider pre-trained embeddings if reasonably appropriate—unlikely if the corpus of interest is in Old English—before proceeding to tune a locally trained model.

Intrinsic tasks evaluate embeddings as models of semantics. These include word analogy—algebraic operations are performed using word vectors to answer questions such as "France is to Paris as Germany is to..."; word similarity—pairs of words along with their human provided similarity ratings are compared to similarity ratings computed using word embeddings; synonym tests—TOEFL multiple-choice synonym questions; noun-clustering—a similarity measure is used to assign words to a pre-defined number of semantic classes; sentence completion (specific to the Skip-Gram architecture)—select from multiple choices to fill in the missing word in a sentence. These tasks require human generated data. Researchers tend to rely on existing datasets that are either freely available online or can be requested from the original authors. However, this can be problematic as existing datasets may be ill-suited to a particular corpus or for a particular semantic relation of interest. For example, word similarity datasets often do not differentiate between the various ways in which two words can be related (Faruqui et al., 2016).[23] Moreover, semantic relationships are likely to vary as a function of demographics (Garimella, Banea and Mihalcea, 2017; Halpern and Rodriguez, 2018*d*), yet few datasets have information on the background characteristics of the subjects. The role of demographics or other background characteristics, including partisanship, is of particular relevance to social scientists. Indeed, these differences are precisely what we are

---

[22]The lack of consensus extends beyond political science (Nayak, Angeli and Manning, 2016).

[23]Agirre et al. (2009) distinguish between similarity—as in coffee and tea—and relatedness—as in cup and coffee. Words can be related syntactically or semantically (Baroni, Dinu and Kruszewski, 2014; Mikolov, Chen, Corrado and Dean, 2013). According to structuralist theory words can have paradigmatic —words that tend to occur in similar contexts— and syntagmatic —words that tend to co-occur— relations (Sahlgren, 2008; Saussure, 1959).

interested in! Below we make the case for crowdsourcing as a flexible alternative allowing researchers to tailor the tasks to specific objectives and gather demographic information when appropriate (Benoit et al., 2016; Schnabel et al., 2015).

We compare models using four criteria:

1. technical criteria —model loss and computation time;

2. model variance (stability)—within-model Pearson correlation of nearest neighbor rankings across multiple initializations;

3. query search ranking correlation—Pearson and rank correlations of nearest neighbor rankings;

4. human preference— a "Turing test" assessment and rank deviations from human generated lists

The latter two criteria can also be used to compare pre-trained embeddings with locally-trained embeddings, which we do. To illustrate this framework, we compare pre-trained embeddings to a set of locally trained embedding models varying in two parameters: embedding dimensions and window-size. Before proceeding with our estimation framework we discuss each criteria in greater depth.

3.5.1   Technical Criteria

The most straightforward metric to compare different models is prediction loss at the point of convergence (i.e. when training stops). There may be theoretical reasons to choose specific values for window-size and embedding dimensions. Given no apriori justification for a given set of values, these may be tuned using model performance. If the intuition motivating `GloVe` is correct, namely that meaning is strongly connected to co-occurrence ratios, then the set of parameter values that optimizes the correspondence between the embedding vectors and the global co-occurrence statistics should produce more "meaningful" embeddings. Generally speaking, larger window sizes and more dimensions both translate into longer computation times, resulting in a performance vs computation time tradeoff. We therefore also compare the set of locally-trained models with respect to computation time in minutes.

3.5.2 Stability

As we discussed above, embedding models are unstable. This is likely to vary for different parameter choices. To quantify this instability we look at the Pearson correlation of nearest neighbor rankings across a set of different vector initializations for each combination of parameter choices. Given ten separately estimated models for a given parameter pair, we have 45 pairwise correlations for each model ($\frac{n(n-1)}{2}$, or the lower diagonal of the 10×10 correlation matrix). We compare the distribution of these pairwise correlations across models. Below we provide more detail as to how we arrive at these samples and the overall estimation framework.

3.5.3 Query Search Ranking Correlation

While prediction loss is informative, it is not obvious how to qualitatively interpret a marginal decrease in loss. Ultimately, we are interested in how a given embedding model organizes the semantic space relative to another. To evaluate this, we appeal to the information retrieval literature. A common objective in information retrieval problems is to rank a set of documents in terms of their relevance to a given query. In our case we are interested in how two models rank words in a common vocabulary in terms of their semantic similarity with a given query term. One potential measure is the intersection over the union (IoU) — also known as the *Jaccard Index*— between the set of top N nearest neighbors for a given target word (see e.g. Pierrejean and Tanguy (2017); Sahlgren (2006)). The problem with using the IoU Index is that it is highly sensitive to the choice of N and there is no principled way of choosing N. Moreover, the IoU does not take into account rank order. There may be cases where the IoU is appropriate—when N is well-defined and order is irrelevant—but for the comparisons below we opt for comparing the entire ranking—all words in the common vocabulary—for a set of predefined query terms. We do so using both Pearson correlation and rank correlation. The higher these correlations, the more similar the embedding spaces of both models. Below we discuss how we went about choosing the query terms.

3.5.4   Human Preferences

The output of distributional models with strong predictive performance need not be semantically coherent from a human standpoint. This point was illustrated by Chang et al. (2009) in the case of topic models. For this reason we make a clear distinction between predictive performance and semantic coherence, and propose separate metrics to evaluate both.

Turing Assessment

To evaluate semantic coherence we draw inspiration from the fundamental principles laid out by Turing (1950) in his classic article on computer intelligence. In that context, a machine showed human-like abilities if a person engaging in conversation with both a computer and a human could not tell which was which. We use that basic intuition in our study. In particular, an embedding model achieves "human" performance if human judges—crowd workers— cannot distinguish between the output produced by such a model from that produced by independent human coders. In our case, the idea is not to "fool" the humans, but rather to have them assert a preference for one set of outputs over another. If a set of human judges are on average indifferent between the human responses to a prompt and the model's responses, we say we have achieved human performance with the model. By extension, a model can achieve *better than human* performance by being on average preferred by coders. Naturally, models may be *worse than human* if the judges like the human output better.

Before getting into specifics, it is helpful to clarify some aspects of the intuition. First, there is a superficial similarity between our approach and more conventional supervised learning problems. This is misleading. In those arrangements, the researcher employs humans to hand-code a training set. Then they use a model to learn the relationships between the covariate features of the data and the class labels given by the humans. After this, the analyst sees how well the machine can predict "held out" human labels in a test set. The machine's performance can then be directly assessed in terms its ability to replicate the human judgments for each case. But this is not what we are doing. Instead, we ask whether humans themselves, on seeing a statistical model's best attempt to describe a concept, find that representation reasonable relative to one produced by other humans. Second, while the Turing test connotes a human versus machine contest, the approach here is more general. Indeed, any output can be compared to any other—including where both sets are produced by a model or both by humans—and conclusions drawn about their relative performance as judged by humans.

The steps we take to assess the relative Turing performance of the models are as follows:

1. **Human generated nearest neighbors:** For each of the ten political prompt words above have humans—crowd workers on Amazon MTurk—produce a set of nearest ten neighbors—we have 100 humans perform this task. Subsequently rank "human" nearest neighbors for each prompt in terms of the number of mentions and choose the top 10 for each prompt.

2. **Machine generated nearest neighbors:** For the embedding model under consideration— pre-trained or some variant of the locally fit set up—produce a list of ten nearest neighbors for each of the ten given prompt words above.[24]

3. **Human rating:** Have a separate group of humans perform a Triad task —135 subjects on average for each model comparison— wherein they are given a prompt word along with two nearest neighbors —a computer and a human generated nearest neighbor— and are asked to choose which nearest neighbor they consider better fits the definition of a context word.[25]

---

[24]It is common in the literature to focus on the *top ten* nearest neighbors. See for example McCarthy and Navigli (2007) and Garimella, Banea and Mihalcea (2017).

[25]See Supplementary Information for the exact wording of the task.

4. **Compute metric:** For each prompt compute the expected probability of the machine generated nearest neighbor being selected and divide by 0.5. This index will range between 0 and 2. A value of 1 implies the embedding model is on par with human performance (i.e. a human rater is equally likely to choose a nearest neighbor generated by the embedding model as one generated by another human).

In most cases there is some overlap in the set of nearest neighbors being compared. The comparisons we show subjects never include the same nearest neighbor for both models; in these cases we assume either model has 50% chance of being selected. This requires we adjust the expected probability of a machine generated nearest neighbor being selected by the probability of the triad task showing the same nearest neighbor for both machine and human. For both tasks above—collecting human generated nearest neighbors and the triad task—we created specialized `RShiny` apps that we deployed on MTurk. For the triad task we paid subjects \$1 to perform 13 such comparisons—one for each of our political prompt words, one trial run and two quality checks; for the word generation task we paid subjects \$3 to generate 10 associations for each of the ten political prompts. The code for both apps is available from our GitHub.

Log Rank Deviations

Using the set of human generated lists we can compare the aggregate human ranking of each nearest neighbor—as determined by token counts—with their equivalent rank on a given embedding space. So for example, if for the query `democracy` the word `freedom` is ranked 3rd according to human counts and 7th according to a given embedding space, we say it's log rank deviation is $\log((7-1)^2)$. We compute this deviation for every token mentioned by our subjects for each of our politics queries and compute an average over the set of queries for every model.[26]

---

[26]It may be worth limiting this to tokens mentioned by at least N subjects, but here we avoid making additional parameter choices.

3.6　Estimation Setup

Obviously, we need a data set on which to operate, and a particular way to model the embeddings. For the latter, as noted above, we choose `GloVe` simply because it seems more popular with social scientists,[27] though we have no reason to believe our results below would differ much under `Word2Vec`.

Below we extend our analysis to other corpora and other languages, but for now we focus in detail on a collection we deem somewhat representative of political science efforts in this area, the set of *Congressional Record* transcripts for the 102nd–111th Congresses (Gentzkow, Shapiro and Taddy, 2018). These contain all text spoken on the floor of both chambers of Congress. We further restrict our corpus to the set of speeches for which party information is available.[28] We do minimal preprocessing: remove all non-text characters and lowercase. Next we subset the vocabulary. We follow standard practice which is to include all words with a minimum count above a given threshold—between 5-10 (we choose 10). This yields a vocabulary of $91,856$ words.[29]

3.6.1　Implementing Choices

We focus our analysis on two hyperparameter choices and all 25 combinations, though to reiterate the framework we lay out is not specific to these parameter pairs:

1. window-size—1, 6, 12, 24 and 48 and

2. embedding dimension —50, 100, 200, 300, 450

To account for estimation-related instability we estimate 10 sets of embeddings for each hyperparameter pair, each with a different randomly drawn set of initial word vectors. In total we estimate 250 different sets of embeddings. The only other hyperparameter choices

---

[27] In particular, the `GloVe` pre-trained available on February 2, 2019 from `https://nlp.stanford.edu/projects/glove/`, for which the training corpus is Wikipedia 2014 and Gigaword 5.

[28] Focusing on this subset reduces our corpus by around a third.

[29] The pre-trained `GloVe` vocabulary consists of $400,000$ tokens.

we make and leave fixed are the *number of iterations* and *convergence threshold*. We set the maximum number of iterations to 100 and a use a convergence threshold of 0.001 such that training stops if either the maximum number of iterations is reached or the change in model loss between the current and preceding iterations is below the convergence threshold. None of our models reached the maximum number of iterations. We set all remaining hyperparameter values at their default or suggested values in the `Glove` software.

3.6.2 Query Selection

Above we explained that a natural auxiliary quantity of interest is the set of nearest neighbors of a given word in the embeddings space. These form the core of our comparison metric in the sense that we will want to know how similar one set of nearest neighbors from one model specification is to another. And, by extension, how "good" one set of nearest neighbors is relative to another in terms of a quality evaluation by human judges. We use two sets of queries: a random sample of 100 words from the common vocabulary and a set of 10 curated political terms.[30]

For the politics-specific queries, we handpicked 10 terms. First, there are concept words that we suspected would be both easily understood, but also exhibit multiple different meanings depending on who is asked: `democracy`, `freedom`, `equality`, `justice`. Second, there are words pertaining to policy issues that are debated by political parties and motivate voting: `immigration`, `abortion`, `welfare`, `taxes`. Finally, we used the names of the major parties, which we anticipated would produce very different responses depending on partisan identification: `republican`, `democrat`. Obviously, these words are somewhat arbitrary; we could have made other choices. And indeed, we would encourage other researchers to do exactly that. Our prompts are intended to be indicative of what we expect broader findings to look like, and to demonstrate the utility of our generic approach.

---

[30]A more systematic approach would compare the entire vocabulary (see for example Pierrejean and Tanguy (2017)). We found this prohibitively expensive and ultimately unnecessary. A random sample of 100 words should approximate well-enough the comparisons of interest.

3.7   Results: Performance Compared

This section reports the results for the evaluation metrics outlined in section 3.5. We begin with the technical criteria.

3.7.1   Technical Criteria

Figure 3.2a displays the mean—over all ten initializations—minimum loss achieved for all sixteen parameter pairs we considered. Consistent with previous work, more dimensions and larger window-sizes both unconditionally improve model fit albeit with decreasing returns in both parameter choices. Except for very small window-sizes (< 6), improvements become marginal after around 300 dimensions. Unequivocally, researchers ought avoid combining few dimensions (< 100) with small window-sizes (< 6). Keep in mind, however, that using more dimensions and/or a larger window-size comes at a cost, longer computation time (see Figure 3.2b). The largest of our models ($48 - 450$) took over three hours to compute parallelizing over eight cores.[31] This seems reasonable if only computing once and having access to several cores, but can become prohibitive when computing over several initializations as we suggest.[32] In this light, the popular parameter setting $6 - 300$ (window size 6, embedding dimensions 300) provides a reasonable balance between performance and computation time.

---

[31] At the time of writing, a standard laptop has 4 cores available. Keep in mind computation time will be a function of the stopping conditions specified—number of iterations and convergence threshold. 100 iterations and a convergence threshold of 0.001 may be considered too conservative.

[32] Unless the researcher has access to a high-performance cluster (as we did) and is able to parallelize.

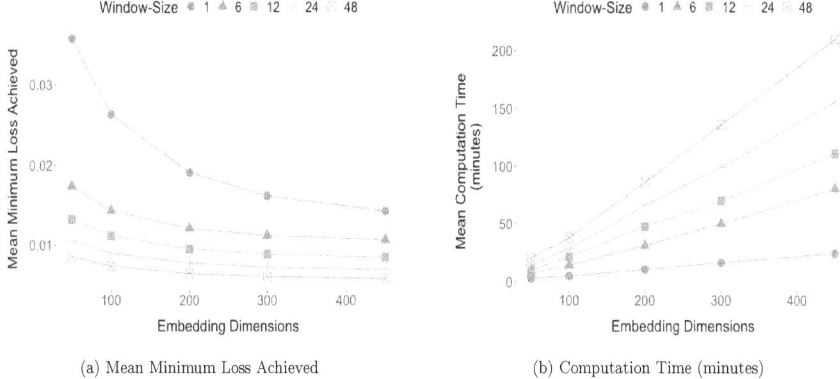

(a) Mean Minimum Loss Achieved

(b) Computation Time (minutes)

Figure 3.2: Technical Criteria

3.7.2 Stability

We next compare all parameter pairs with respect to the stability of the resulting embeddings. Figures 3.3a plots the distribution of Pearson correlations for the 100 random queries. Models with larger window-sizes produce more stable estimates—higher average Pearson correlation and lower variance—but only up to a point. As the number of dimensions increase, the difference in stability between different window sizes decreases and eventually flips—larger window sizes result in greater instability. This parabolic relationship between window-size, number of dimensions and stability is likely a function of corpus size and token frequency.[33] For the set of 10 politics queries we observe the same trends although do not reach the point at which the relationship reverses (see Figure 3.3b).

---

[33]For the State of the Union, a much smaller corpus below, we find the flip occurs after 100 dimensions.

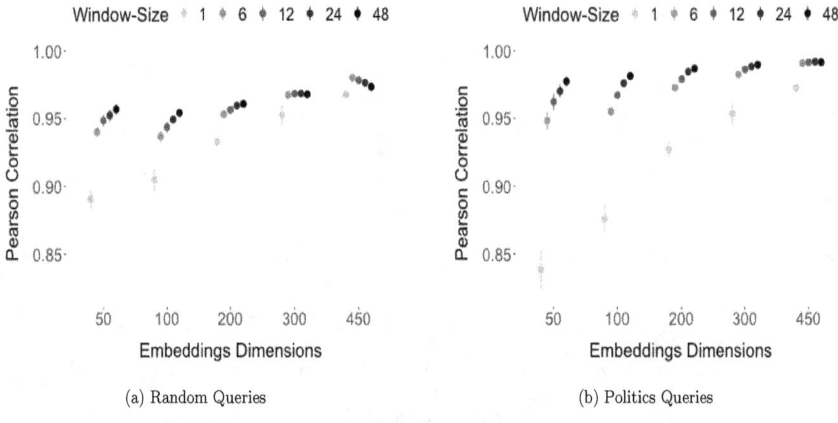

(a) Random Queries (b) Politics Queries

Figure 3.3: Stability Criteria

3.7.3 Query Search Ranking Correlation

Clearly different parameter choices produce different results in terms of performance and stability, but what do these differences mean substantively? To answer this question we turn to comparing models with respect to how they rank query searches. Figure 3.4a displays a heatmap of pairwise correlations for all models, including GloVe pre-trained embeddings, for the set of random queries.[34] We observe high positive correlations (> 0.5) between all local models. Correlations are generally higher between models of the same window-size, an intuitive result, as they share the underlying co-occurrence statistics. Somewhat less intuitive, comparing models with different window-sizes, correlations are higher the larger the window-size of the models being compared (e.g. 6 and 48 vis-a-vis 1 and 6). Correlations are larger across the board for the set of political queries (see Figure 3.4b). These results suggest the organization of the embedding space is most sensitive to window-size but this decreases quickly as we go beyond very small window-sizes (i.e. models with window-size of 6 and 48 show much higher correlation than models with window-size of 1 and 6).

The last column of Figures 3.4a and 3.4b compare GloVe pre-trained embeddings with

---

[34]As pre-trained embeddings we use the 6-300 GloVe embeddings.

the set of local models. For this comparison we subsetted the respective vocabularies to only include terms common to both the local models and the pre-trained embeddings.[35] As would be expected, correlations are lower than those between local models, yet they are still surprisingly large—especially for local models with larger window-sizes and for the set of political queries (all above 0.5). Our reading is that GloVe pre-trained embeddings, even without any modifications (Khodak et al., 2018), may be a suitable alternative to estimating locally trained embeddings on present-day political corpora. This is good news for political scientists who have already relied on pre-trained embeddings in their work.

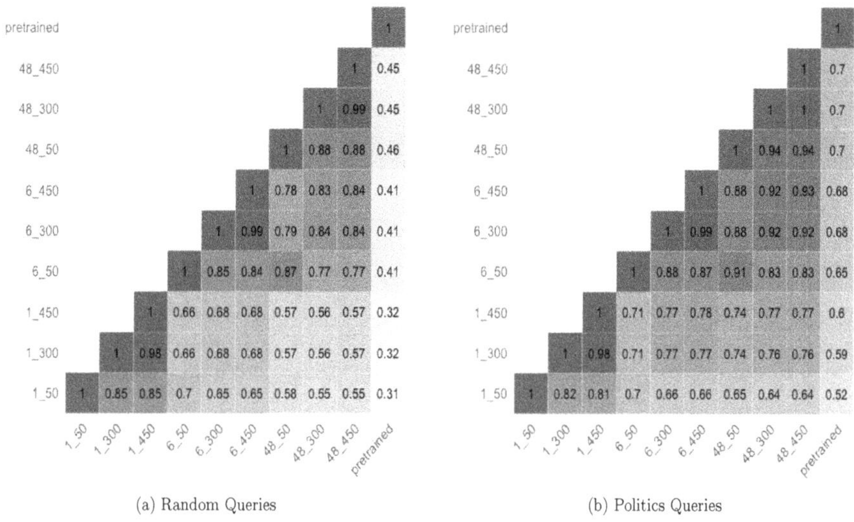

(a) Random Queries   (b) Politics Queries

Figure 3.4: Query Search Ranking Criteria

As a final check, we looked at whether pre-trained embeddings might do a 'worse' job of reflecting highly specific local embeddings for our focus corpus. In this case, we mean party: it could in principle be the case that while pre-trained embeddings do well in aggregate for the *Congressional Record* they do poorly for Democrats or Republicans specifically. To evaluate this we estimate a set of additional local models (again, 10 for each group and using 6-300 as parameter settings) for subsets—by party—of the aggregate corpus. We find

---

[35]In the appendix we include additional comparisons without subsetting the vocabularies.

no statistically significant differences in correlations for the politics queries (see Supporting Information.).

3.7.4 Human Preferences

Recall that human raters represent our gold-standard evaluation metric, and we assess performance here on two different types of tasks.

3.7.5 Turing Assessment

Figures 3.5a– 3.5d measure performance of a "candidate" model relative to a "baseline" model. Recall, values above (below) 1 mean nearest neighbors from the "candidate" model were more (less) likely to be chosen by human raters. A value of 1 means human raters were on average indifferent between the two models. Figure 3.5a compares two local models: $48 - 300$ (candidate) and $6 - 300$ (baseline). There is no unqualified winner. We see this as consistent with previous metrics—these models have a 0.92 correlation (see Figure 3.4b).

How do local models fare against human generated nearest neighbors? Except for one query (immigration), the local model of choice—6-300—shows *below-human* performance for all but two of the queries. On average, for the set of ten political queries, the local model achieves 69% (std devn= 0.20) of human performance. Turning to pre-trained GloVe embeddings, we observe that they are generally preferred to locally trained embeddings (see Figure 3.5c). Moreover, pre-trained embeddings are more competitive against humans—albeit with greater variance—achieving an average of 86% (std dev $= 0.23$) of human performance.

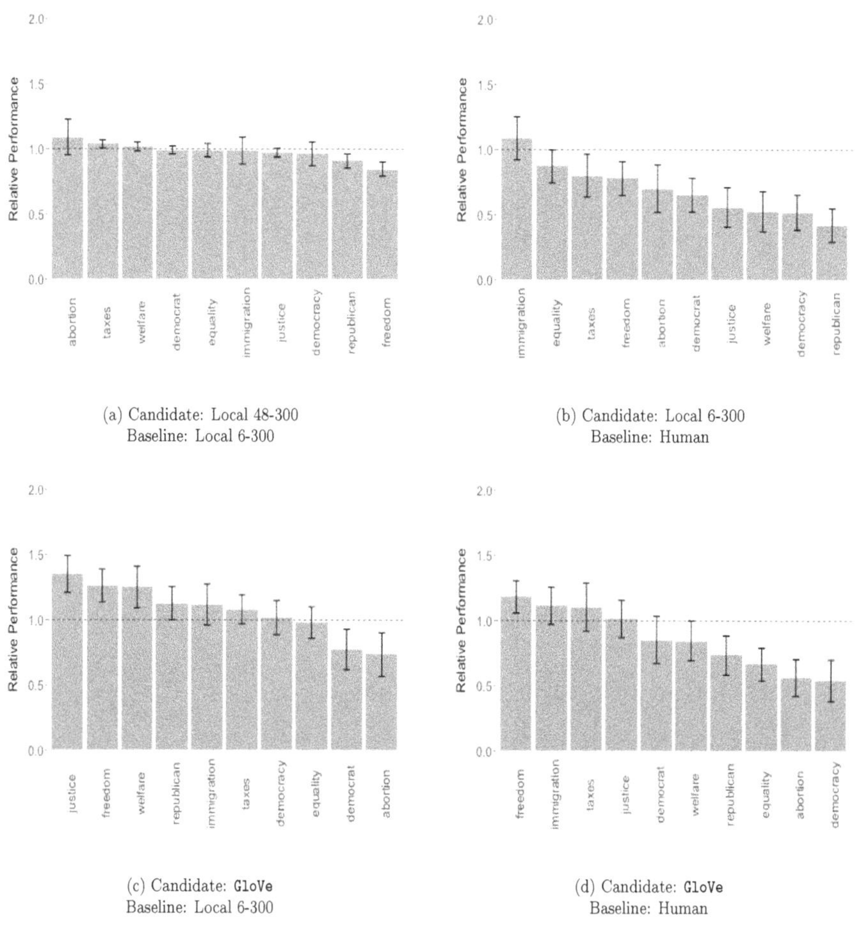

Figure 3.5: Human Preferences-Turing Assessment

3.7.6 Log Rank Deviations

Using the log rank deviation measure, we can compare all models given our set of human
generated lists (see Figure 3.6). Results generally mirror those obtained using our technical
loss criterium, barring the large confidence intervals. Models with larger windows and more
dimensions show lower log rank deviations, indicating better performance but with decreasing
returns. This suggests a strong correspondence between predictive performance and semantic

coherence as hypothesized by the distributional hypothesis.

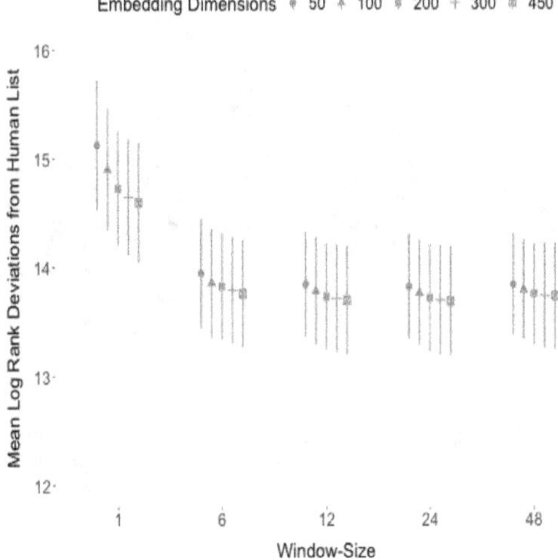

Figure 3.6: Human Preferences-Log Rank Deviations

3.8   Other Corpora, Other Languages

Our core results presented, we now extend our evaluation to four other corpora, varying in size and language. These are:

1. the full set of speeches from the UK Parliament for the period $1935 - 2016$

2. all State of the Union (SOTU) speeches between 1790 and 2018

3. the full set of speeches from both chambers of the Spanish Legislature —*Cortes Generales*— for the V - XII legislatures.[36]   As political queries we use: `democracia, libertad, igualdad, equidad, justicia, inmigracion, aborto, impuestos, monarquia, parlamento`.

4. the full set of speeches from the German Legislature—*Deutscher Bundestag*— for the election periods 14 - 19.[37] The political queries in this case are: `demokratie, freiheit,`

---

[36] As the XII was ongoing at the time of writing we used all speeches available up until Oct-18.

[37] As the 19th *Wahlperiode* was ongoing at the time of writing we used all speeches available up until Oct-18.

`gleichberechtigung`, `gerechtigkeit`, `einwanderung`, `abtreibung`, `steuern`, `cdu` and `spd`.

We did not find readily available pre-trained embeddings in German, as such all our comparisons in this case are between locally trained embeddings. Both the Spanish and German corpora are original datasets collected for the purposes of this paper.[38]

Table 3.2 provides summary statistics for these corpora and the *Congressional Record* corpus. We can see that the SOTU corpus is substantially smaller than all the other corpora and also encompasses a much longer time period.

Corpus	Period	Num. of Docs.	Num. of Tokens	Avg. Tokens/Doc.	Vocab. Size
Congressional Record	1991 - 2011	1,411,740	3.4×10^8	238	91,856
Parliamentary Speeches	1935 - 2013	4,455,924	7.2×10^8	162	79,197
State of the Union	1790 - 2018	239	2.0×10^6	8143	11,126
Spanish Legislature	1993 - 2018	1,320,525	3.0×10^8	224	94,970
German Legislature	1998 - 2018	1,193,248	0.8×10^8	69	108,781

Table 3.2: Corpora Summary Statistics

In the Supporting Information section, we provide the same results plots as we gave for our *Congressional Record*. Perhaps surprisingly, but no doubt reassuringly, these are almost identical to the ones above. That is, when we look at the embedding models we fit to these very different corpora, the lessons we learn in terms of hyperparameter choices, stability and correlations across search queries (i.e. on the issue of whether to fit local embeddings, or to use pre-trained ones) are the same as before. Of course, there are some exceptions: for example, we do find models of window-size equal to one perform well in the case of the SOTU corpus and for the German corpus—though to a lesser extent.

3.9   Advice to Practitioners

In this section we summarize our results in terms of what we deem the main takeaways for practitioners looking to use word embeddings in their research. First, in terms of 'choice' parameters in applied work:

---

[38] We have made these publicly available, and these may be downloaded via the project's github page.

- **Window-size and embedding dimensions:** with the possible exception of small corpora like the State of the Union speeches, one should avoid using very few dimensions (below 100) and small window-sizes (< 5), especially if interested in capturing topical semantics. While performance improves with larger window-sizes and more dimensions, both exhibit decreasing returns—improvements are marginal beyond 300 dimensions and window-size of 6. Given the tradeoff between more dimension/larger window-size and computation time, the popular choice of 6 (window-size) and 300 (dimensions) seems reasonable. This particular specification is also fairly stable meaning one need not estimate multiple runs to account for possible instability.

- **pre-trained vs local embeddings:** `GloVe` pre-trained embeddings generally exhibit high correlations (> 0.4 for the set of random queries and > 0.65 for the set of curated queries) with embeddings trained on our selection of political corpora.[39] At least for our focus *Congressional Record* corpus, there is little evidence that using pre-trained embeddings is problematic for subdivisions of the corpus by party—Republican vs Democrat speech.

  Human coders generally prefer pre-trained representations, but not for every term, and it is quite close for many prompts. Specifically, `GloVe` pre-trained word embeddings achieve on average—for the set of political queries—86% of human performance and are generally preferred to locally trained embeddings.

  These results suggest embeddings estimated on large online corpora (e.g. Wikipedia and Google data dumps) can reasonably be used for the analysis of contemporaneous political texts.

  Further, if one does wish to train locally, the computational overheads are (not especially) severe, at least for a medium size corpus, so this is probably not a reason *per se* to use pre-trained embeddings.

---

[39]This is lower in the case of small corpora like the State of the Union, and in the case of random queries for the Spanish corpus.

Second, in terms of methodology lessons on *how* to evaluate models:

- **Query search:** in the absence of a clearly defined evaluation metric—a downstream task with labeled data—embeddings can be compared in terms of how they "organize" the embedding space. We propose doing so using query search ranking correlations for a set of randomly selected queries and—given a specific domain of interest— a set of representative domain-specific queries. To discriminate between models resulting in very different embedding spaces, both can be compared to a baseline, either a model known to perform well or, as we do, a human baseline.

- **Crowdsourcing:** Crowdsourcing provides a relatively cheap alternative to evaluate how well word embedding models capture human semantics. We had success with a *triad task* format, a choice-task with an established track-record and solid theoretical grounding in psychology.

- **Human "Turing" test:** a given embeddings model—or any model of human semantics for that matter—can be said to approximate human semantics well if, on average, for any given cue, the model generates associations (nearest neighbors) that a human does not systematically prefer to human generated associations.

  Specifically, we define human performance as the point at which a human rater is indifferent between a computer and a human generated association.

Third, in terms of 'instability'

- **Stability:** word embeddings methods have a lot of moving parts many of which introduce an element of randomness into the estimation. This produces additional variability beyond sampling error which, if unaccounted for, can lead to mistaken and non-replicable inferences. To account for estimation-related instability we endorse estimating the same model several times, each with different randomly drawn initial word vectors and use an average of the distance metric of choice.[40] The good news, from

---

[40]Note, all packages initialize word vectors randomly so this simply amounts to estimating the same model several times.

our results at least, is that embeddings that perform well on the technical and human metrics tend to also be the most stable. Finally as an aside, the embeddings themselves should *not* be averaged as they lie in different spaces.

3.10   Discussion

Word embeddings are well on their way to being widely adopted by political scientists. We see this as a positive trend. However, it is often the case with technology transfer that adoption far outpaces understanding. It is our goal in this paper to preempt this outcome. In addition to a brief introduction to the history of embeddings and the inner workings of three popular models, we have provided practitioners with a framework to perform model comparison and validation. This includes both technical and substantive criteria, including a new Turing-style test that pits humans against 'machine' in the generation of meaningful associations to a given cue. Applying this framework to a set of representative political science corpora, varying in both size and language, we generate a series of takeaways that will hopefully aid practitioners get a head start in the application of embeddings for their research. Our results can generally be considered good news for political scientists: by all the criteria we used, off-the-shelf pre-trained embeddings work very well relative to— and sometimes better than—both human coders, and more involved locally trained models. Furthermore, locally-trained embeddings perform similarly—with noted exceptions—across specifications which should reduce end-user angst about their parameter choices. We stress that the framework we propose is not confined to the evaluation of embeddings but rather can be used to evaluate any model of semantics including cross-model comparisons. Finally, of course, we have focused on *relative* performance: we have not studied whether embeddings are interesting or useful *per se* for understanding behavior, events and so on. We leave such questions for future work.

Supporting Information for Chapter 3

C.1: Task Wording

Context Words

A famous maxim in the study of linguistics states that:

You shall know a word by the company it keeps. (Firth, 1957)

This task is designed to help us understand the nature of the "company" that words "keep": that is, their CONTEXT.

Specifically, for a CUE WORD, its CONTEXT WORDS include words that:

- Tend to occur in the vicinity of the CUE WORD. That is, they are words that appear close to the CUE WORD in written or spoken language.

AND/OR

- Tend to occur in similar situations to the CUE WORD in spoken and written language. That is, they are words that regularly appear with other words that are closely related to the CUE WORD.

For example, CONTEXT WORDS for the cue word COFFEE include:

1. *cup* (tends to occur in the vicinity of COFFEE).
2. *tea* (tends to occur in similar situations to COFFEE, for example when discussing drinks).

Click "Next" to continue

(a) Context Words

Task Description

For each iteration of the task (13 in total including trial and screener tasks):

1. You will be given a cue word (top center of the screen) and two candidate context words (on either side of the cue word).

2. Please select the candidate context word that you find best meets the definition of a context word.

3. We are especially interested in context words likely to appear in **political discourse.**

4. If both are reasonable context words, please select whichever you find most intuitive.

5. You must select **one and only one** of the two candidate context words.

Keep in mind, some iterations are for screening purposes. These are tasks for which there is clearly a correct answer.

Wrong answers in these screening tasks will automatically end your participation so **be sure to read carefully.**

The trial task that follows is meant for you to practice. Like screening tasks, the trial task has a correct answer.

Click "Next" to continue to the trial runs

(b) Task Instructions

Figure 3.7: Instructions

C.2: Jaccard Index

To further evaluate the correspondence between pre-trained embeddings and local models we use the average Jaccard-index —also known as the intersection over the union (IoU)— over the set of random and politics queries (Pierrejean and Tanguy, 2017; Sahlgren, 2006). The Jaccard-index between two models for a given query corresponds to the number of common nearest neighbors in the top N (the intersect of the two sets), over the union of the two sets. For example, take the following two sets of top 5 nearest neighbors for the query word **democracy**: $A = \{$freedom, democratic, ideals, vibrant, symbol$\}$ and $B = \{$freedom, democratic, dictatorship, democratization, socialism$\}$. Given two nearest neighbors in common, the IoU is $\frac{|A\cap B|}{A\cup B} = \frac{2}{8} = 0.25$. Figure 3.8 plots the Jaccard-index, for various values of N, between GloVe pre-trained embeddings and several local models varying by window size. Unlike with the Pearson correlations we do not subset the respective vocabularies. As with the Pearson correlations, we observe larger values as window-size increases but with decreasing returns.

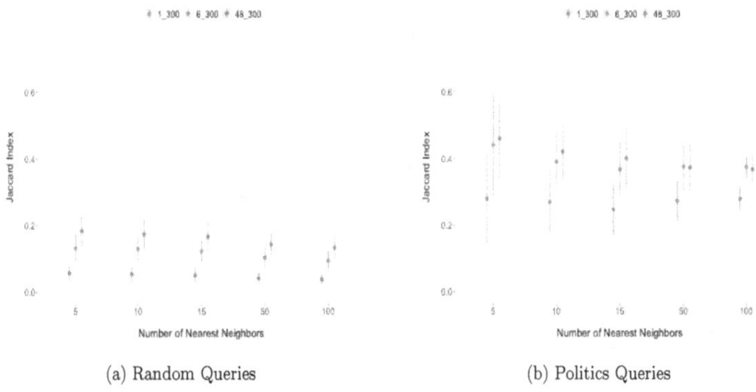

(a) Random Queries
(b) Politics Queries

Figure 3.8: Jaccard Index Between pre-trained and Local Models

C.3: Window size and discrimination for a real corpus

The claim is that larger windows mean that we can better discriminate between term meanings. We looked at the evidence for this on our *Congressional Record* corpus. To assess the claim we first set up a set of 'true negatives'—words that should be (fairly) unrelated. In particular for us, these are just random pairs of words from our corpus. We also evaluated how the average distance varies for 'true positives', that is words that are in fact the same. To assess this we sampled 100 words from the vocabulary. Suppose `congress` is one of those 100 words. We then...

1. tag half of the appearances (randomly selected) of `congress` in the corpus as `congress_tp`. So, if `congress` appears 10,000 times, in our transformed corpus it will appear as `congress` 5000 times, and `congress_tp` 5000 times.

2. estimate a set of embeddings with the vocabulary including both `congress` and `congress_tp`.

Now we have an embedding for `congress` and `congress_tp`. These should be close in embedding space, since they are the same word albeit (randomly) half the incidences have been given a different token (hence we call them "true positives"). We interpret *how* close they are as measure of performance.

In Figure 3.9a we plot the mean difference in similarity terms between the true positives and the true negatives. When this number is large, we are saying similar words look much more similar to one another than random words (i.e. our model is performing well). When this number is smaller, the model is telling us it cannot distinguish between words that are genuinely similar and words that are not. On the left of the figure, fixing the embedding dimensions at 300, we see that larger windows translate to bigger differences—i.e. the model performs better in terms of discrimination. We call this *meaningful separability*.[41] As an aside, on the right of the figure, we see that for a fixed window-size of 6, increasing the number of dimensions actually causes the model to do worse.

---

[41] Keep in mind, removing words from a corpus prior to processing into input-target pairs effectively enlarges the window-size (Levy, Goldberg and Dagan, 2015). This need only really be of concern when interested in syntactic relationships which requires smaller windows.

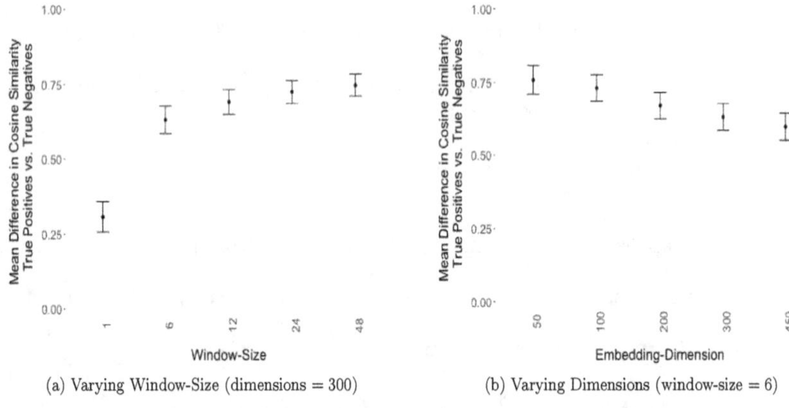

(a) Varying Window-Size (dimensions = 300)   (b) Varying Dimensions (window-size = 6)

Figure 3.9: Mean Difference in Cosine Similarity True Positives vs. True Negatives

C.4: Pre-trained embeddings perform equally across subgroups for *Congressional Record*

Above we showed that overall GloVe pre-trained embeddings correlate highly with locally trained embeddings. Next we ask whether these correlations differ by party. Such biases can be problematic if pre-trained embeddings are subsequently used to analyze texts and draw conclusions on the basis of party. To evaluate whether pre-trained embeddings exhibit bias we compare query search results based on pre-trained embeddings to results based on locally trained embeddings specific to each group (Democrat and Republican legislators). We say pre-trained embeddings exhibit bias—according to this metric—if query search results correlate significantly higher with the query search results of one group relative to the other.

This evaluation requires we estimate separate embeddings for each of these groups. To do so, we split the congressional corpus by party (Republican vs Democrat). We apply the same estimation framework as laid out in section 3.5 to each sub-corpora except we fix window-size and embedding dimension at 6 and 300 respectively.

Figures 3.10a and 3.10b display the main results of our evaluation for a random set of queries and our set of politics queries respectively. For neither set of queries do we find evidence of partisan bias—as defined here—in pre-trained embeddings.

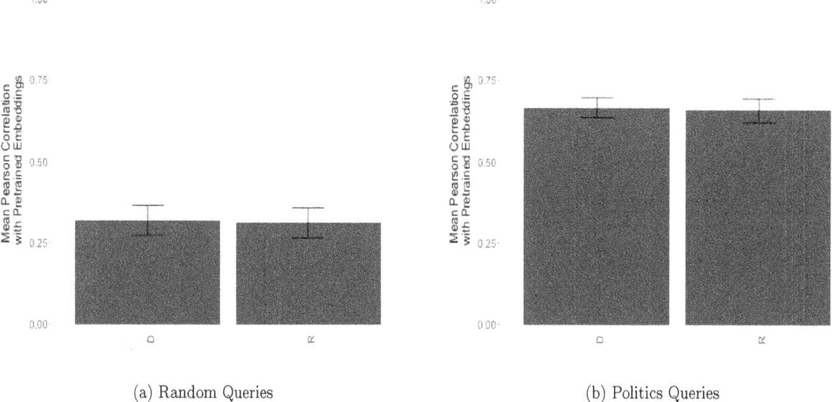

(a) Random Queries

(b) Politics Queries

Figure 3.10: Pearson correlation of group embeddings with pre-trained `GloVe` embeddings.

C.5: Other Corpora, Other Languages: Results

C.5.1: Technical Criteria

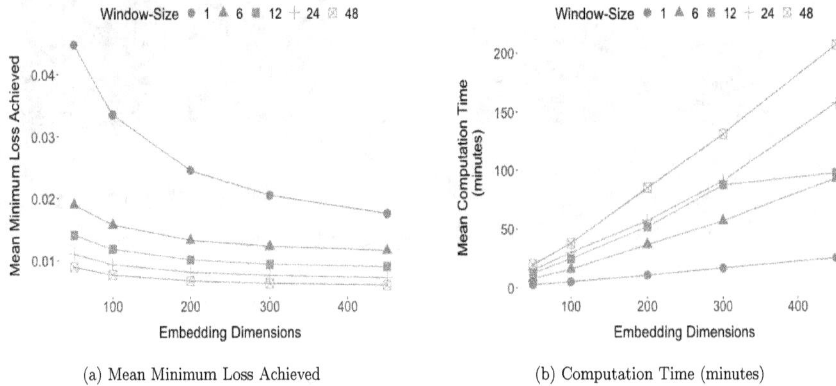

(a) Mean Minimum Loss Achieved   (b) Computation Time (minutes)

Figure 3.11: Technical Criteria: Parliamentary Speeches

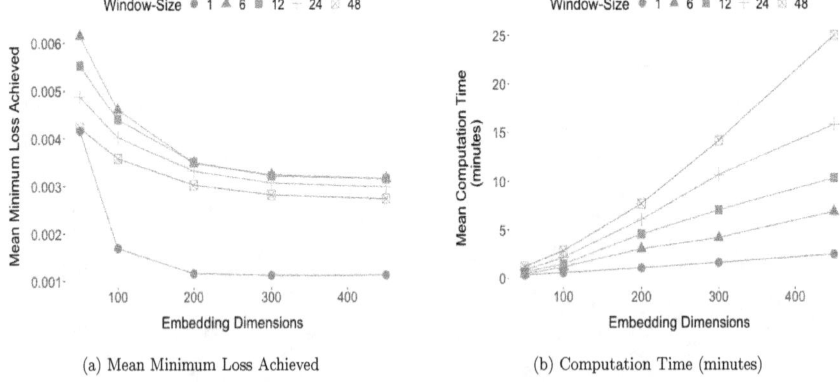

(a) Mean Minimum Loss Achieved   (b) Computation Time (minutes)

Figure 3.12: Technical Criteria: State of the Union Speeches

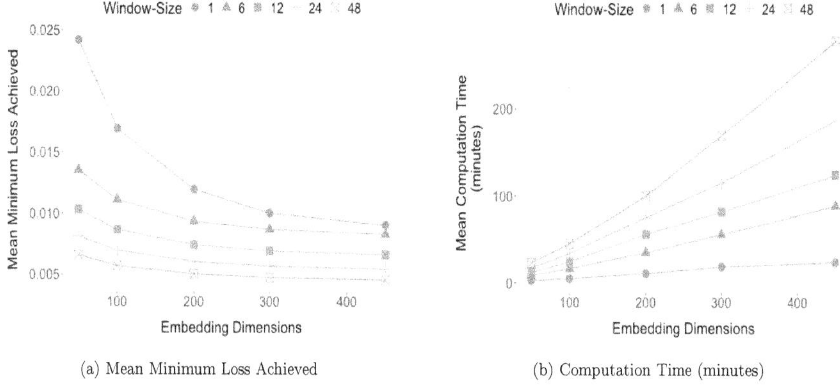

(a) Mean Minimum Loss Achieved

(b) Computation Time (minutes)

Figure 3.13: Technical Criteria: Spanish Corpus

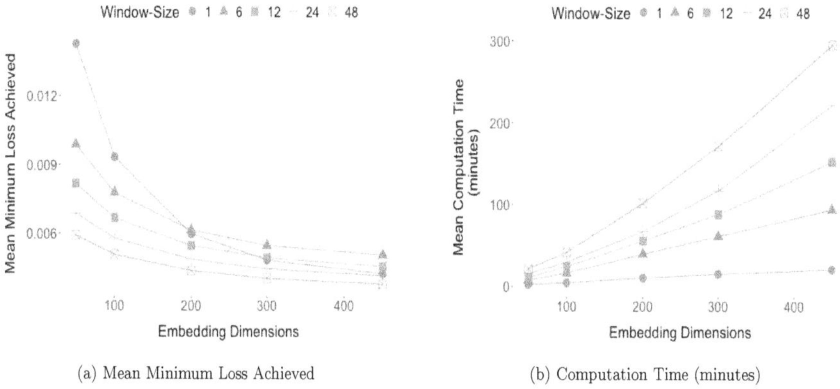

(a) Mean Minimum Loss Achieved

(b) Computation Time (minutes)

Figure 3.14: Technical Criteria: German Corpus

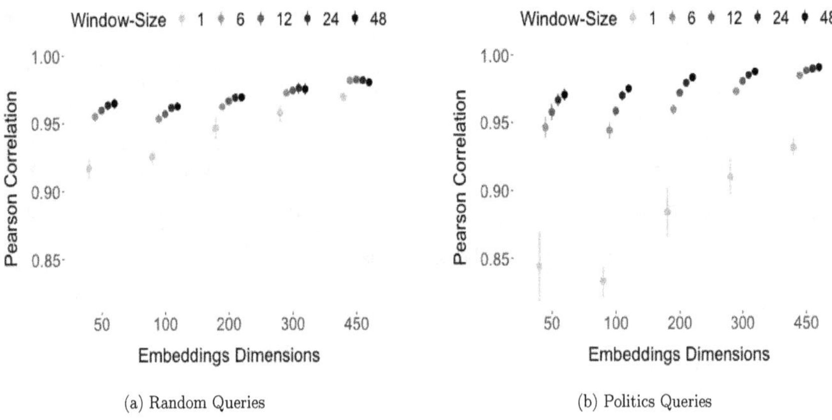

(a) Random Queries   (b) Politics Queries

Figure 3.15: Stability Criteria: Parliamentary Speeches

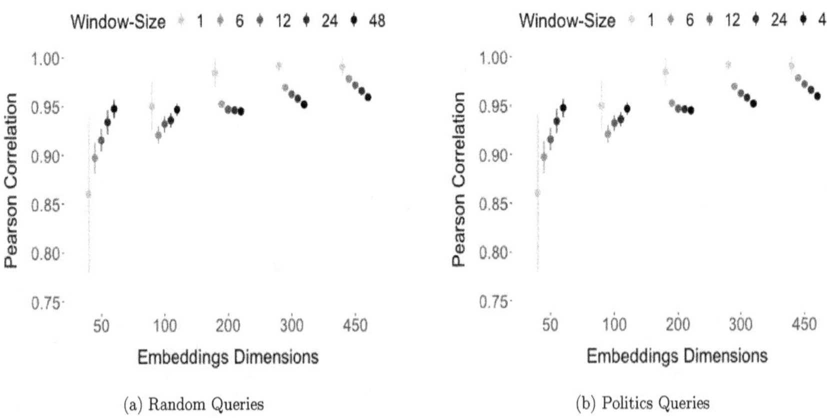

(a) Random Queries   (b) Politics Queries

Figure 3.16: Stability Criteria: State of the Union Speeches

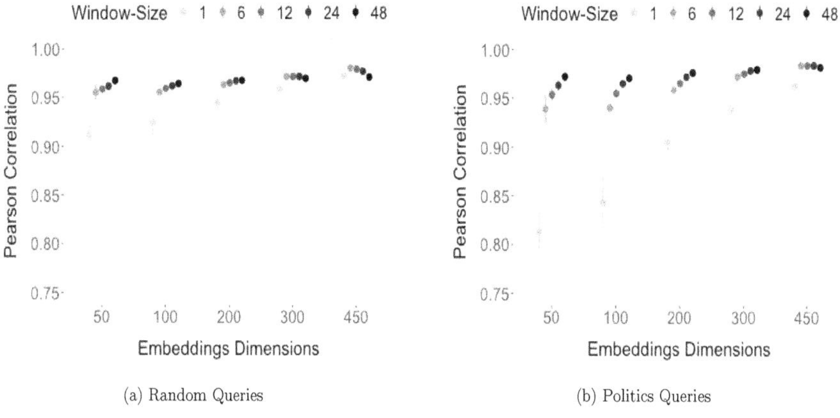

(a) Random Queries

(b) Politics Queries

Figure 3.17: Stability Criteria: Spanish Corpus

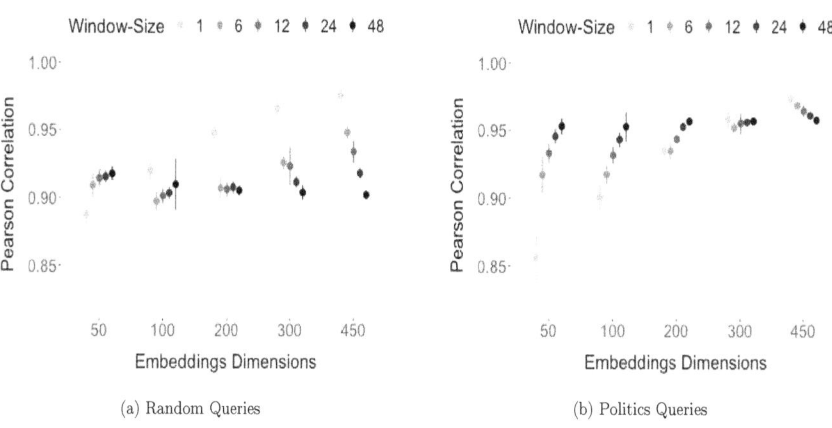

(a) Random Queries

(b) Politics Queries

Figure 3.18: Stability Criteria: German Corpus

C.5.3: Query Search Ranking Correlation

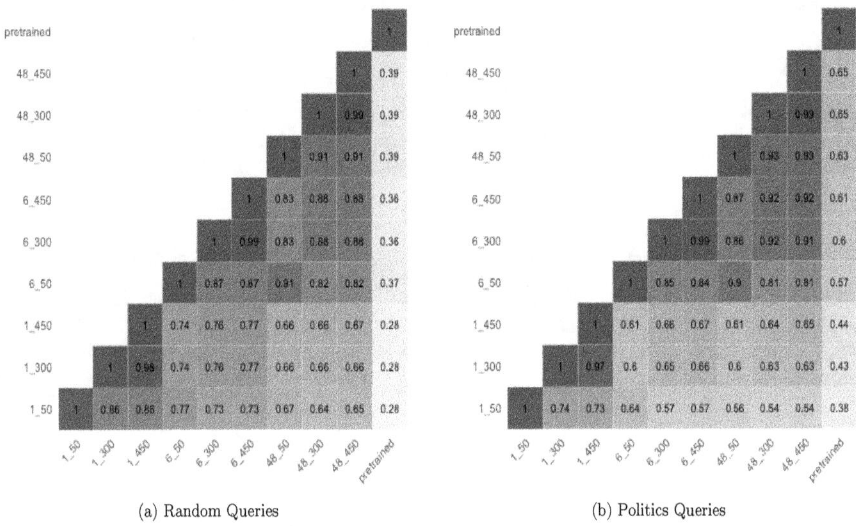

(a) Random Queries   (b) Politics Queries

Figure 3.19: Query Search Ranking Criteria: Parliamentary Speeches

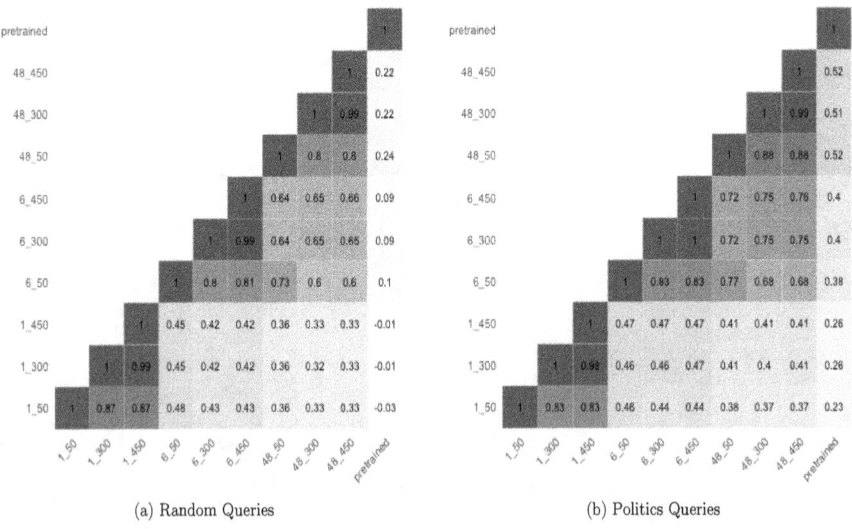

(a) Random Queries   (b) Politics Queries

Figure 3.20: Query Search Ranking Criteria: State of the Union Speeches

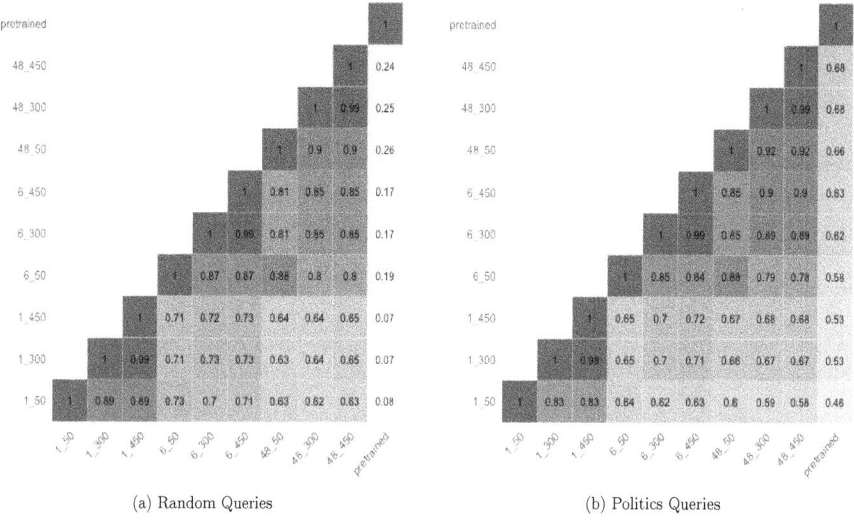

(a) Random Queries

(b) Politics Queries

Figure 3.21: Query Search Ranking Criteria: Spanish Legislature

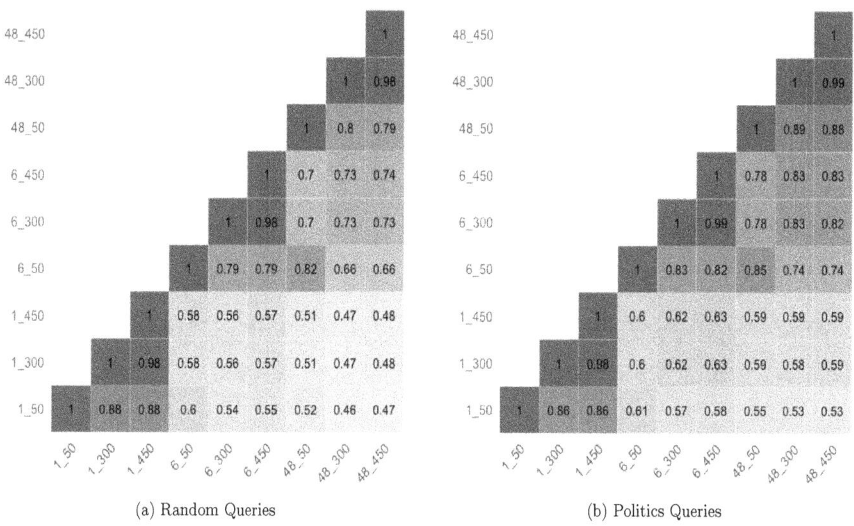

(a) Random Queries

(b) Politics Queries

Figure 3.22: Query Search Ranking Criteria: German Legislature

C.5.4: Human Validation

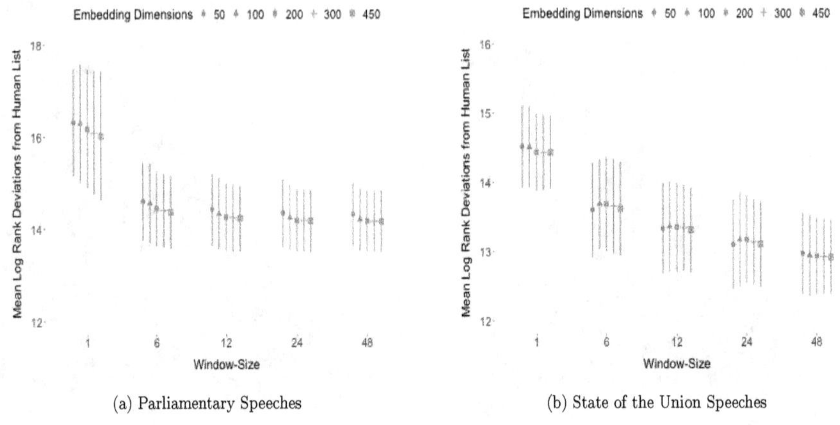

(a) Parliamentary Speeches   (b) State of the Union Speeches

Figure 3.23: Human Preferences-Log Rank Deviations